Getting There

Getting There

the first thirty years, 1935-1964

Charles Shere

…músico y peregrino y significativo…

CERVANTES

ISBN 978-0-6151-5935-5

Printed in the United States of America

Contents

snapshots

…nothing without Lindsey…

In my mother's arms, 1935

1: Berkeley and Before, 1935-1945

DAD WORKED IN A SAWDUST FACTORY when I was born. In fairness, he had only recently turned twenty-four himself, and he was late to find his trade. And in those respects I copied him, in spades: I was just nineteen when my first child was born, and didn't settle into a decent profession for another ten years.

He worked in a sawdust factory; it says so on my birth certificate. I suppose this is incomprehensible today. What's a sawdust factory? Why would anyone work in one? Sawdust today is simply the necessary byproduct of sawmills, wherever they are; and it has no visible presence in our daily life, unless you look under the veneer of your cheap furniture.

But I was born in 1935, when sawdust was genuinely useful in daily life. It still covered the floors of butcher shops in those days, because butchers still cut up whole carcasses in those days, and things spilled on the floor, and sawdust was easily swept up at the close of the day. Ditto taverns and barrooms, I suppose, though I didn't see any until a few years later, when Dad would bring me with him into this place or that at the end of the workday on the special summer occasions that he took me into town for the day, there to wander the stationery shops and the bookstores and the specialty household emporia that offered me a glimpse into an exotic and sophisticated way of life quite unlike that we knew at home.

And sawdust was needed by the iceman. The iceman still came around every few days, stopping when the tattered diamond-shaped placard was set in the window, 25 or 50 or 75 or 100 showing at the top, so that he could bring the right size on the first and only trip he made to the back stairs.

I should say quickly that I recall that detail from later, and not from my own house, I mean my parents', but from my grandparents'. I have only the haziest memories of childhood apart from my grandparents until I was in high school. And in fact it's my grandparents' address that's given on my birth certificate: 1817 Bancroft Way, Berkeley, California.

My mother was the second daughter and, I think, the third child of a family of nine children, and her father was a professional man with reliable employment during the difficult Depression days: he taught physics and chemistry in high school. They had settled in Berkeley because he had gone to college there. In fact one of my last memories of him is the procession he headed, as the oldest living graduate, into the ancient, oracular Greek Theater on Commencement Day, in the late 1970s, with my own oldest daughter, then herself a college student, on one side, and me on the other. I suppose my mother was there as well: four generations, extending the collected memory present far into the past, and well into the future, if only symbolically.

It's that collected memory that seems increasingly important to me now, as I approach seventy. It becomes clear that any individual life is essentially meaningless, leaving aside the Homers and the Shakespeares and the Mozarts of human history; that it's in the continuity of these meaningless individual lives that any lasting interest lies. The continuity across the years, which are the subject of history and memory; and the continuity within a given time and place, which animates that sense of present belonging that is so ordinary and necessary as to lack any common name that I can think of, and goes in my own language by the exotic and poetic phrase genius loci.

So I contemplate Dad in his sawdust factory, Berkeley 1935, just as I hope my grandchildren would one day, trying to find some meaning in it. The expression "sawdust factory" was a new one to me when I first read it on that birth certificate. When was that, I wonder? Probably in 1973, when I first applied for a passport. As with so many other things I never gave it a moment's thought. My mind was on impressions from outside, not inside — outside myself, my family, my own immediate surroundings. The familiar experiences were all too drab, it seemed to me. Well, not really drab; simply ordinary and devoid of interest.

Now, though, now when it's far too late to get any eyewitness explanations or recollections of life in those sawdust factory times, Dad's daily business in that factory seems immensely interesting. I know only that what he actually did there was sew up burlap sacks. Whether he manufactured them, or repaired them, or simply sewed them closed once they were filled with sawdust, that I do not know. (The last, I suppose.) Nor do I know how I know that is what he did: someone, Mom or Aunt Dorothy or maybe Aunt Barbara, must have mentioned it idly one day, a nugget of information that was interesting only for its absurdity — a grown man spending his day sewing up gunny sacks. How I wish I could pursue this further now!

I don't know why or how I know this, but I'm certain the sawdust factory was in fact the coal-wood-and-feed store that stood in those days on the north side of University Avenue, a few blocks west of Grove Street. My own world centered on Bancroft and McKinley, quite a few blocks south of University. It was at that corner that my grandparents' big white box of a clapboard twostorey house stood, with its enormous bay tree on one side, down Bancroft to the west, and the Chinese neighbor's house on the other, up McKinley to the north.

I don't recall straying any further from this center than one trip to a Mexican restaurant on University Avenue, the only restaurant meal I can recall our family ever taking; and, an equal distance in the other direction, a visit my grandmother paid to a genteel but poor friend, probably a church friend, who lived down near Ashby Avenue, where my grandmother said only the Irish lived; but Mrs. Scoggins must not have been Catholic, or my grandmother would have been unlikely to have known or visited her.

Why would my grandparents' address have been given as my parents' on my birth certificate? I suppose my parents were between houses of their own. My first ten years were a succession of moves from one place to another, and I suppose the five years before my birth were no different. Certainly Dad had been on the road for a long time. He was born in Oklahoma, but his family moved when he was very young to Bisbee, on the Mexican border in Arizona, where his father worked in the mine until the day when, desperate I suppose in poverty and trapped in marriage and fatherhood he left my grandmother, my other grandmother I'm talking about now, to shift for herself and her three kids.

By then Dad had finished the sixth grade, so he went to work to help support the family. One way or another things worked out. Uncle Alvie, Dad's kid brother, finished high school and got a job with the Atchison Topeka & Santa Fe Railroad, where he worked until his retirement. My aunt, Dad's kid sister, died of a ruptured appendix when she was only eight or nine years old. I of course never saw her, and never heard much about her, but her photograph is in my bedroom, a pretty, vivacious, attractive little girl full of promise. Her death had no meaning beyond its contribution to Grandma's growing sense of good-humored courage in the face of constant sadness and need.

¶¶¶

Shift of locus, from Berkeley to Carmel, where Mom and Dad converged in the early 1930s. They're at the beginning of their adult lives, by which I mean they are more or less independent from their own parents. I know how and why Dad arrived in

Carmel: he road the freight trains there, part of the Okie migration during the Great Depression. I think he sought his fortune out of a different need than the one that drove most of those hapless dust-bowl farmers and small-town tradesmen, though. They were driven by the sheer need to survive; he was led at least in part by wanderlust. Abject poverty was in his bones; he'd already survived that. He was optimistic and cheerful by nature, at least until later on when guilt and anger distorted his personality, and I'm sure he expected to find an unimagined and perhaps unimaginable grown-up life of his own.

Isn't this what was meant in those days by such old-fashioned words as "vocation" and "calling"? The meaning of a man's life in those days was what he *did*; it was the meaning he gave to his position within his family and his community by the contributions he made with his daily work. The Depression called into question the meaning of all but the very richest of the rich. The middle classes were led, many of them, certainly the most sensitive of them, back to the question of community and one's individual address, you might say, to one's community. There wasn't much question of attaining significance by growing rich or amassing belongings. The quality of one's daily life — how one filled time, what one found to eat, the conversations one had with one's friends — this essentially social quality of life must have assumed the priority given in other periods to the acquisition of things, or the distractions of travel, or the attainment of manipulative power.

Carmel, like Berkeley, changed greatly in the last two thirds of the twentieth century. I think the two towns had more in common then, in the Depression years. At least Carmel, with its bohemian arts-and-crafts life, had much in common with a part of the Berkeley of those days, and not the part of which my mother's parents would have necessarily approved. In any case Mom was a romantic in those days; we still have her early poems to prove it. They suggest an intelligent young woman who read Sir Walter Scott and was in love with landscape. (I write this partly out of projection, I know: but it's fair to extrapolate backward as well as forward in pursuing Meaning through memory and connectivity. Generations and Drift will be my constant subject here for a few pages, as I try to situate myself within the inexorable continuity of family and place.)

Carmel and its bohemian community was an island of refuge in the dreary poverty of the Depression. Mom had gone there as a friend of her older sister Olive, and with other school friends no doubt, to get away from her own parents, and Church, and the difficulty of finding work — though she did work in Berkeley for a while, as a waitress I suppose, at an eating-place called Drake's, which served students and faculty at the University.

Dad had gone there because he had two aunts he must hardly have known, sisters of his father's, who lived in Pacific Grove. I do not know how or why they settled there, or even what their surnames were, Smith or Shere or names taken through marriage; but I remember visiting Gladys and Myrtle (what characteristic names!), fifty years ago or so. I think one of them had something to do herself with crafts — a potter, perhaps? In any case he settled with them temporarily and found a job dishwashing or perhaps cooking in a Carmel hash-house, where Mom was waitressing for a time.

There are periods of social stability, like the Eisenhower years, and periods of instability; inhale and exhale, systolic and diastolic.

¶¶¶

I write this partly in order to attempt a mediation of such swings: the Law of Excluded Middles always offended me. Childhood is necessarily self-centered, and "growing up" is the exploration of the periphery. To be an adult, I suppose, is to resolve the differences of self and community. That resolution depends on a conversation, not an orderly debate, between the principals. "Among," not "between," for the community speaks with a thousand voices.

I was lucky, in my first ten years, to grow up within an extended family. I wasn't to meet my Oklahoma grandmother, Grandma, until I was nine years old; and I don't think I ever met her absent first husband, even though he lived (and died) not far away from Berkeley, in Grass Valley, still a miner.

I can't tell now, so many years later, whether I really remember having seen a mysterious man in a heavy overcoat — itself a strange sight in Berkeley, where it was never really cold — or whether I simply remember having been told about him, a poor man sent out west on the train, his name and history written on a sort of baggage-tag tied to a coat-button. This would likely not have been my grandfather but an even more mysterious man, his father, Charles Smith of Kansas, who is buried in a veteran's grave somewhere in Central California, having died, I suppose, obscure and unlamented, in a home for aged veterans in the 1930s.

(A note on the family name: for whatever reason the three children of Charles Smith were raised by a family named Shere, and they took that name, probably more as a matter of course than through any legal structure.)

But if my father's parents were mysteriously absent, my maternal grandparents were ever-present. The first residences I remember were within a few blocks of their house on Bancroft Way. There was a curious cottage in the middle of the block, between Roosevelt Street and McGee, Allston Way and Bancroft, where I recall my uncle Bobby trying to teach me to tie my shoes, sitting on a bench in the sun on the front porch.

There was an apartment, I suppose, on the west side of Grant Street I think, still between Bancroft and Allston, where I recall our having a pigeon-loft of some sort in a screened-in porch on the back side of the building — I'm sure we raised the pigeons for meat; squab was a favorite of Dad's, and must have appealed to the peasant-but exotic streak in Mom. And I seem to recall a car at the curb in front of this apartment: but whose?

By now Dad must have left the sawdust factory and begun working as a car mechanic for Mr. Jensen, the old Dane who ran a garage up near Telegraph Avenue. Perhaps Mom was working then at Drake's, and I was spending most of my time at Gram's; that's a reasonable assumption.

In any case there was a trip out to Mr. Jensen's home one day, probably a springtime weekend — I recall flowering fruit trees. Mr. Jensen lived on a few acres out in Castro Valley, not yet transformed from such smallholdings to its present configuration of tract houses and shopping centers. We drove out in a coupé, as they still said in those days, a coupé with a rumble seat, and there was a long dirt driveway it seemed, among those fruit trees, and then Mr. Jensen and his wife in her apron, smiling in a front yard of some kind, chickens here and there I believe. I don't know why we were there; I'm sure the Jensens were not close friends of my parents. I do remember once Mom showing me a letter from Mr. Jensen, undoubtedly before we moved from Berkeley, though most likely after Dad stopped working for him — or why would he have written? Mom found it difficult to read, and she explained to me that it was written in a different kind of hand than the cursive we all used, me too, for I was taught to read and write ahead of the normal schedule; Mr. Jensen's hand was spindly and scrawly though curiously regular, and Mom explained that it was the kind of writing the Germans used.

Mom was fond of languages, having grown up exposed to three — English at home, Cantonese with the amah, French with the other kids at school — and she enjoyed dabbling with them, and was fond of singing simple songs, or reciting bits of things, in German or French. I recall Gramp had a similar habit, falling back on stock phrases in Scots dialect, or Latin, or Chinese, though as far as I know his own childhood was transacted in no language but English.

Mom was born in Canton and spent her childhood in Shanghai and, for a brief period, in Nanking. Her parents had gone to China right after the birth of their first child, my aunt Olive. Gramp had met Gram in Fresno, where he was posted as a teacher after graduating from the University. I suppose they met through the church, as both of them came from solid Protestant families. But family legend has it that Gram's mother was domineering, and Gramp decided he had to get away from her, no doubt in order to keep his family together on his own terms. The first distant job to come up was in China, where he taught physics and chemistry in Chinese schools, and where they lived in one or another of the many foreign "missions" then sprinkled about the larger cities, established to support trade missions, religious conversion being a convenient adjunct to the confused transition then in place between the traditional imperial colonialism and the incipient global economy.

While in China Gram gave birth to eight more children: after Olive, born in Fresno, there was Clay, Peg (my mother), Charles, David, Mary, Bob, Barbara, and Dorothy. And then they returned to the States. On hearing the news of the death of the mother-in-law they took passage via Yokohama and Seattle and settled in Berkeley at 1817 Bancroft, and Gramp got a job teaching chemistry and physics at Mission High School in San Francisco, and the rhythm of his working life was established, rarely to vary until his retirement.

Five days a week Gramp commuted via streetcar and ferry to his work, and on Saturdays he made some extra money painting and papering. I don't know where he picked up those skills, but I do know where he found his customers: at church, most of them. And, perhaps because of his long residence in China, he found many among the Chinese community in Berkeley, then quite extensive. When we bought our own house, Lindsey and I, on Curtis Street, in 1973, I immediately recognized its wallpaper, and Gramp confirmed that he had in fact hung it, years ago, for the Tang family, friends of Homer Lee, who gardened for the Christian Church of which Gramp was a deacon, and who had a florist shop next to the socially experimental but then far from left-wing Consumers Cooperative of which Gramp was an early member.

Christmas 1941: (l-r) Ricky, CS, Claudia, Jim; Gram and Gramp behind

How complex the politics of the Depression must have been! And how subtly they must have intruded on our family, Mom's family I mean, already so hopelessly complex and varied. At 1817 Bancroft I remember aunt Dorothy, only a dozen years older than me, tanning herself on the "sun porch," really the roof of the front porch, conveniently accessible by a window off the staircase. Uncle Bobby was always either absent or in traction in his bedroom, one leg or another in a cast suspended from the ceiling, having broken it in another motorcycle accident, usually in the gravel on Fish Ranch Road up in the Berkeley Hills.

The other aunts and uncles were rarely seen, appearing at Christmas and Thanksgiving and at the weddings that seemed to punctuate those Berkeley years. Olive's was the first I remember, to a foreign-looking man with a mustache, George Orly, whose own family was whispered to be of Hungarian stock. (Gramp and Gram were charitable, but the moral superiority of British stock and American protestantism was never in question.) Olive and George lived unimaginably far away, up in the Berkeley Hills near the reservoir, in a new house that seemed impossibly modern and luxurious to me, all windows and daylight with a concrete floor covered with rugs. Olive always had refined tastes. There was a grand piano, I don't know where it came from, and low sofas, and lots of books — the first book I remember reading was their copy of James Thurber's *The Last Flower*, which seemed impossibly sad and romantic; this would have been in 1944 or so. (I had already been reading, of course; I'd read children's series like the *Uncle Wiggly* titles and I particularly liked another, *The Curly-tops*, about a boy with tightly curled white hair just like mine when I was four or five; I liked to tear the dog-eared corners off the pages and chew them ruminatively while reading.)

In 1942 they produced another cousin, Roxanne; and she very early was subjected to ballet lessons, and there I heard recorded classical music, and began to associate it with dance of a sort. But I was already taking piano lessons, in a studio in the aboveground basement of the church across Bancroft from my grandparents. Did I practice, if I practiced at all, at home? I don't remember a piano in the apartment we had for a while at the southwest corner of Allston and McKinley, down the block from Gramp's, where I remember spending days in bed with the whooping cough. It seems unlikely we would have had a piano at that early date, or space to house one. I don't remember a piano in the apartment we had for a while at the southwest corner of Allston and McKinley, down the block from Gramp's, where I remember spending days in bed with the whooping cough. I must have practiced at Gram's, on the piano that was a wedding gift to her from her parents, and which sailed to China and back with them, and kept its place in their home even into the late 1950s, when I was yet again to take refuge with them...

It may have been Mr. Jensen's example that led us to settle for a few months in Lafayette, then a sleepy town out to the east of the Berkeley Hills. We had a place in the country, in a walnut orchard; I don't know if we rented it or had somehow bought it or were more likely simply squatting it for a few months. Here I had my first automobile accident: I had dragged a good many of the kitchen chairs, and my tricycle, and whatever else I could out to make a sort of train behind the trailer Dad had fashioned out of a pickup-truck bed and a spare axle. The trailer was already attached to the rear bumper of the family car, which Dad had left parked on a gentle slope among the trees. I got behind the steering wheel and somehow managed to release the brake, and the car rolled backward, smashing all the chairs and finally crunching the trailer into a walnut tree.

¶¶¶

Yes, George Orly was exotic; I later heard that he worked, at the time Mom and Dad met in Carmel, in a "garlic factory" — no doubt a plant processing garlic salt — in Gilroy. Sawdust factory, garlic factory: conversions of whole natural phenomena into small particles of only fugitive usefulness. That must have been quite a community of expatriate Berkeleyans (and one Okie from Bisbee): Olive and George, Mom and Dad, aunt Mary and Joe Swift, the man who'd marry her, father her five children, and then years later leave her for a younger woman...

They worked the garlic, sewed gunny sacks, cut firewood, hunted frogs, waited tables, washed dishes. Mom tinted photographs for a time, and carved cameos. I have no idea how or where or when she developed those skills. I always took her drawing and her poetry for granted, an took equally for granted her renunciation of such things as we moved from Berkeley, to wartime Richmond, back to Berkeley, then to Oklahoma, finally to The Ranch.

The history of those relocations is a clearly outlined curve in my mind, from the blurred mysteries of the beginnings of memory in Berkeley to a more poignant and uprooted year in Richmond, back for a reassuringly bourgeois year in Berkeley, then to a confusing deracination in lowerclass Welch, Oklahoma, and finally to the denial that constituted our farm, if you can call it that, in Sonoma county, where Mom and Dad longed for self-sufficiency, and I longed for escape.

And the history centers on that great interruption of recent history, the Second World War. I first heard about it on December 7, 1941. We were moving into a new house, a detached two-bedroom cottage with white walls and a green roof at 242 Twenty-fifth Street, and Dad was trying to get a highboy through the doorway into one of the bedrooms, when Mom called out excitedly from another room: *The Japs have bombed Pearl Harbor! My God, the Japs have bombed Pearl Harbor!*

Never mind the goddam Japs, Dad shouted back at her, *Come help me get this goddam thing through this doorway!*

By then there were four of us. After five years of being an over-indulged only child I was now an older brother. I remember Dad driving us across the bridge to San Francisco, where we parked on a side street from which he pointed to a window high up on the side of the University hospital: Mom was there, waving. I had been born at Berkeley General Hospital, no doubt with financial help from Gramp, but Jim was born at the University hospital, where twenty years later I would have teeth extracted, unable to afford a private dentist.

A younger brother was not yet more than a minor distraction from life as I'd known it. Nor do I recall other children at school. There was a red-headed girl who socked me in the eye on the playground at Washington School, where I spent half a year in kindergarten, the remaining half in first grade, for already Mom was interfering with the normal course of public education, insisting that I was being held back from my own intellectual pace. In December 1941 I began the second grade, in Richmond, and of that I recall nothing but the playground, again more for loneliness and exclusion than because of any childhood friendships.

I remember more vividly excursions away from home and school, early explorations of that periphery: I ran away to Nichols Park, several blocks distant, and lost myself in fascination with the caged monkeys and exotic birds. In those days even a town like Richmond, not yet plunged by wartime economy into the social and economic unrest that's marked it ever since, maintained such gentilities as municipal aviaries, places where the innate American fascination with the beyond and the frontier could be not only satisfied but further stimulated. And more poignantly I remember another exploration, when I spent a half hour sliding down the concrete abutment of a railroad overpass, wearing out the seat of my pants and requiring me to run home with my hands clapped to my exposed rear end.

And there was a Circus, suddenly flowering among its tents on a previously empty lot; and immediately after leaving the circus a surprise trip to a hospital to have my tonsils out, where I recall withdrawing my right hand from its restraint, while going under the ether, and socking an innocent nurse with a small but defensive fist...

¶¶¶

Everyone in Mom's family married exogamously, and the boys left home for as distant an alternative as possible, all but uncle Bobby, immobilized by his frequent tractions, and uncle Charles, already dead of creeping paralysis. Charles was almost never mentioned. He had been named for his father, as I had been named for mine; but I often wonder if Mom weren't attracted to Dad partly because of his name.

(Oddly neither my father nor Mom's went by his first name. Gramp's name was Charles Ellis, but he was called Ellis, a practice that had begun in his own childhood to distinguish him from his own father, Charles Burton. And my father, Charles Everett, was known as Everett for the same reason: his father was Charles Edward. Mom's middle name was Ellistine, which she never mentioned, though she always signed her name "M.E. Shere." And in my own family our youngest daughter married a man whose given name was that of her own brother...)

My mother must have been preoccupied with the news from Pearl Harbor: her brother Clay was in the Philippines at the time. I remember seeing uncle Clay off on a beautiful sunny day, the glamorous white and blue Pan-American Flying Clipper tethered to a dock at Treasure Island, Clay in a white linen suit and a Panama hat, confidently walking toward the stairs into the cabin. He flew back to Manila, where he put my aunt Dottie and my cousins Joanne and Claudia on the last ship out; and then he spent the next four years in a prison camp.

Treasure Island was where I played my first concert, at the World's Fair. The island had been created out of dredged materials from the Bay, originally with the idea of being a new airport, but soon to be taken over by the Navy and Coast Guard for wartime use. In the meantime it was the site of the 1939-1940 Pan-Pacific Exposition, with palm trees and fountains, elaborate stucco exposition halls and gayways, and "elephant trains," trains of open cars drawn by gasoline-engine tractors made to look like cartoon elephants, to transport fair-goers among the attractions on this really quite extensive island, as big as a small city.

There I played violin in an orchestra of school-children. I remember only three things: the sound of one piece, perhaps the only piece we played, "Kitty-cat Waltz," featuring occasional glissandi between adjacent notes; and the little girl next to me embarrassingly and distractingly and inexorably wetting herself out of pure anxiety; and the sounds of occasional gunshots from, I was later told, the nearby Sally Rand Dude Ranch, which of course I never saw.

The childhood memories of sounds: a subject that interested me years ago when I wrote a biography of my own composition teacher, Robert Erickson. Stravinsky recalled the sound of the ice breaking in the Neva. Erickson recalled — what? I'd have to look it up. I recall the Kitty-cat Waltz, and gunshots, and Gram crooning to me as she rocked me on the front porch on warm afternoons on Bancroft Way.

ain't you the limit
ain't you the limit

I recall the crackling flames and terrifying shouts accompanying the burning of Atlanta, in the movie *Gone With the Wind*, sitting between Mom and Dad and smelling the coffee they'd brought with them in a big Thermos bottle; and I recall Mom and Dad yelling to each other on Pearl Harbor Day, 1941.

Richmond, 1942

Why Richmond? Dad had left the sawdust factory years before, having taken a trade-school course in sheet metal working, then a job at a factory that made Pullman cars for the railroad. Of course I know very little about all this, but much later I remember looking at his textbooks and marveling at the production of boxes, cylinders, and complex cones from simple sheets of metal. I suppose he worked on the heating and air-conditioning systems in those Pullman cars. Once we drove past the factory, a huge sprawling building on a rise beyond the railroad tracks that paralleled the main road skirting the Bay leading from Berkeley to Richmond.

The War brought big changes. Mom began to work, too, first taking welding classes, then working in one of the many Kaiser shipyards quickly established along the Richmond waterfront. Dad worked on the Liberty ships as well: his poor eyesight disqualified him from military service, a severe disappointment to him, perhaps also to Mom.

At some point Dad suffered a potentially serious injury at work: an overhead crane lost its grip on a sheet of steel, which fell to the ground. Dad, either to protect himself or someone nearby, raised his hand instinctively to deflect it, getting a nasty gash on his hand. He was taken for First Aid to the shipyard sick bay, from which Kaiser Permanente would eventually evolve; but blood poisoning set in, and he had to soak his arm frequently in Epsom salts, whose chemistry fascinated but mystified me.

In his spare time Dad was a Block Warden, responsible for maintaining defensive alertness among the residents of our block. There were frequent practice blackouts lest Japanese bombers were to fly over, a real fear in those days. Once or twice a month, I suppose, there were block warden meetings upstairs in the old brick firehouse in the old part of town, Point Richmond, and I would be admired by the other men, most of them probably grandfathers by then, when Dad occasionally took me with him.

I don't know if my piano lessons continued; I certainly don't recall a piano in the house. I walked to my violin lessons, given in another brick building, a storefront around the corner from home on McDonald Avenue; but before long these lessons stopped, and my violin succumbed to an experimental launching in the bathtub, perhaps inspired by one of the almost daily launchings in the shipyards. I used to blame this experiment on my brother Jim, but I'm no longer so sure it wasn't my own fault.

Richmond was an isolating experience in many ways, at least for me. There couldn't have been many visits back to Berkeley, except I suppose for weekends. Mom and Dad made new friends at the yards, and I remember going with them to more than one dance party, where couples jitterbugged and two-stepped in a brightly lit hall to the big-band tunes of the day — recorded, I suppose, since live musicians would have left an impression with me. But the comfortable adult friends back in Berkeley were rarely seen, and I was still too young to have made any lasting friends of my own age. After a year we moved back to Berkeley, perhaps for this very reason, but a pattern had been set, and this alternation of isolation and community would continue until I was grown up.

Berkeley, 1943

The house at 1517 North Street is the first I remember in any real detail, though we lived there only a year and a half. It was a real house in a real neighborhood, a twostorey brown shingle house with a gable roof, on the north side of a blind street only half a block long, with similar houses around it, and fully grown trees, the first I'd lived with apart from the huge bay tree at Gramp's. There were delightful secret passages under the gables, their excitement enhanced by the pungent smell of old fir and dust and the insulation of the knob-and-tube wiring — I think I can even smell the porcelain of the insulating tubes, flinty and chalky at the same time. We had our own bedroom, Jim and I, at the back of the house, and outside the window was the broad leafy head of an enormous tree, a sycamore or a maple I would imagine.

In the back yard, alongside the detached garage filled with junk — another interesting jumble to explore on rainy days — we had our vegetable garden and a small chickenyard, for everyone in those days raised as much food at home as possible. There was an apricot tree, and berry bushes. There were other kids to play with, though since I don't remember them specifically I must have kept my distance, or they theirs. There were my two cousins Joanne and Claudia only two or three blocks away, in a similar house perched high up on a bluff, as it then seemed to me, living with Aunt Dottie and her mother, waiting out the war and hoping for the best for Uncle Clay.

Across the street from their house there was a corner grocery store, where I used to gaze at one lone can of sliced pineapple on a high dusty shelf — Mom used to make a wonderful pineapple upside-down cake, but with the War on such commodities were forbiddingly expensive, not in terms of money perhaps, but in terms of the paper stamps and pressed-fiber "coins" that governed traffic in such rationed items as shoes, gasoline, sugar, and other imports.

I couldn't have known it at the time — I was only seven — but we were Northsiders now. Berkeley is divided, by the university campus and by its only four-lane east-west street, into North and South; South was where the less fortunate classes lived. I don't know how we happened to settle on North Street, but Gramp's brother Percy had some connection with real estate, and may have been involved. (I believe he had something to do with our finding The Ranch, a couple of years later.)

Being on the North side I was sent not back to Washington School but to Whittier, then a model demonstration school, with student teachers from the University, the latest approved textbooks and curriculum, and what seemed to me a marvelously modern new building. I must already have noticed the few tentative experiments in modern architecture in Berkeley, generally so conservative and idiosyncratic in its architectural tastes. There was the round-ended flatiron house climbing a hillside lot between Hearst and Ridge Road; I was entranced with its curves, its steel-framed industrial windows, and its improbably flat roof, every Sunday, when we passed it on our way to church. There was the huge theater building at the high school, a circular cage of steel beams against the sky, its completion stopped by the wartime requisition of materiel. And there was the streamline Art Deco white concrete Whittier School, the lettering of its name recalling the Art Deco typography of Treasure Island and its world's fair, the occasional glass-block window-lights connecting it to the style of that round-ended house on the way to church.

One of the innovations at Whittier was a much more sequestered kindergarten, with its own playground separated from that of the older children, and its smaller furniture and its emphasis on readily available picture books in low accessible bookshelves, and its story hour and the naps the children took on their floor-mats. Why should this be so strong a memory? Perhaps Jim was already in attendance, though he would have been only three years old at the time — though there may have been some kind of child-care there for mothers working in the war effort. Certainly Claudia would have been there. I was now finishing the third grade, whose only residue in memory is the rebuke given me when instead of drawing a duck, as I had been told to do, I drew a duck followed by two or three ducklings. This provoked another visit of my mother to the school authorities, following which I must have been left to myself, as I recall nothing else. Not quite true: I remember the teacher's face; she had sweet brown eyes and curly dark hair.

That summer, the summer of 1943, must have been spent largely back on the south side of town, in my grandparents' neighborhood, where I got into mischief. Years before, these explorations were safely hand-in-hand with my grandmother, on her visits to the neighbors — on one such visit I was frightened by a dog, and ran round and round my grandmother, further exciting the poor thing until it jumped up on me and accidentally clawed my bare belly; I carried the scar for years, and remained leery of big dogs for a long time.

Now, though, I was turning eight years old, and my explorations took me further, sometimes as far, somehow, as the bay shore, where with another boy I looked for things washing up, crates of K-rations and such that had been thrown overboard to see if they'd float, I suppose. Other excursions were to much nearer treasures, like the boxes of canceled checks we found one day in the crawl space under Gramp's house; and the discarded imperfectly blown test-tubes and Erlenmeyer flasks behind the laboratory apparatus factory down Grant Street.

The adult world was a total enigma, its mystery enhanced by the war. The sky to the west, over the bay, was clouded with barrage balloons, tethered to prevent any intrusion of low-flying aircraft. I knew, somehow, that there was a giant steel net suspended across the strait underneath the Golden Gate Bridge, to prevent submarines entering. The Bay was busy with shipping regardless, of course, and I often wondered how they opened and closed that net to accommodate it.

Gramp's car, an old green Hudson I think, was up on blocks in the low-ceilinged garage under the bay tree, and I used to spend hours in its back seat, reading. I did errands for the family, making frequent trips across the street to the little grocery store to buy Cokes for Aunt Dorothy. The parade of weddings had continued: Aunt Barbara married another Bob, one who looked a little like Uncle Bobby, dark and stocky and quiet, and they moved off to a mysteriously remote place in the forests of northern California. Aunt Mary, proud in her newly won nurse's cap and Boston accent, married Joe, who promptly took her off to Texas to his training camp. Aunt Dorothy, who worked at the telephone company, married Lester, who also went away, to London, where, Gram was relieved to hear, he was kept away from the front, his business acumen too useful in the Quartermasters Corps, we were told, to be put in danger.

Uncle Dave was not present — nor, frustratingly, my cousin Rick, only a year or so younger than I. They were up in Santa Rosa, where he'd married a local girl and had insinuated himself into the banking business, probably through his skills on the basketball court and the automobile back seat. It must have been that summer that we visited him and his family, both in Santa Rosa, where I coveted Rick's wonderful electric train — a very large one, perhaps already thirty years old and previously Dave's — and in a summer cabin on the Russian River, where I discovered a trove of old issues of *Esquire* magazine, charming for their hillbilly cartoons, oddly fascinating for the drawings of scantily clad girls (I knew there was something dangerous about them, but had no idea what it was), and above all enticing for the sophistication of such things as instructions on the correct fashion accessories for men, how to tie a Windsor or Four-in-hand knot, and the proper drinks to mix, all things suggesting Life in a City and A World at Peace.

This was far from the daily reminders of what was going on. I don't know that we were indoctrinated directly, but there were always bombing and fire drills at school, and serious conversations among the grownups, and airletters from distant uncles, occasional words heavily blacked out; and there were the frightening photographs in the window of the laundry down at the corner. And the posters: A Slip of the Lip Can Sink a Ship. We Can Do It. One Down (a crude cartoon of Mussolini, a big X drawn across his pudgy face) Two to Go (even cruder cartoons of Hitler and Hirohito).

There were other indications, if I'd been old enough to understand them. Before we moved to Richmond a number of the houses near Gram and Gramp's had fish-ponds in their neatly gardened back yards, with fat carp complacently swimming in them; after we'd moved back to Berkeley the neighborhood seemed different. The Japanese families were gone, and other people had moved in. The low ornamental iron fences were gone from front yards. Trucks came by to pick up newspapers that we carefully baled and set out on the sidewalk; and once I remember I pulled my coaster-wagon along in unfamiliar neighborhoods, collecting the bacon-fat that people saved in tin cans at the back of the kitchen stove; I turned it in to some central store-front, not understanding that it ultimately found its way to munitions factories.

And then one day there was a serious conversation between Mom and Dad: his stepfather, his mother's second husband, had been crushed under a tractor in a road-maintenance accident. Grandma was a nurse, and resigned to tragedy and difficulty, but clearly needed help. We all bundled into the family car, a Ford station wagon with wooden doors, and set out for Oklahoma.

It was now the summer of 1944, and I was nearing my ninth birthday. I was halfway through the fourth grade, still stuck in the half-year school rhythm Mom had insisted on back in kindergarten — a rhythm that had oddly been respected by the Richmond and Berkeley school systems. I can't imagine what was in Mom's mind: just thirty-four years old, she was leaving her parents, her brothers and sisters, and Edith and Sarah, the two special friends she'd had from college, or perhaps from Carmel. She was leaving Berkeley, with its bookstores and music lessons, and going to Oklahoma, then still known primarily for its recent dust storms. She must have already met Grandma, though I don't recall ever having seen her, and I'm sure she liked her — everyone liked her; but she inhabited an entirely different world, and Mom would be imprisoned within it as well, for how long?

Of course the invasion of Europe had already been well begun, and the end of the war must have seemed closer; the Battle of the Bulge had not yet interfered, with its enormous losses delaying the march on Berlin. I think there was even an optimistic mood as we loaded the car: we were setting off on our own adventure, crossing half the country on two-lane roads, many of them badly maintained, in an overloaded station wagon, Jim and me and our long-haired toy shepherd Butch perched on an improvised mattress atop boxes and suitcases and pots and crates, and a big basket of apricots from our backyard tree.

In retrospect I think there was something in Berkeley, or perhaps in Richmond, that we were deliberately leaving. Mom had finally set aside her obsession with my development, perhaps in order to save her own, to remove the family from some threat I was too innocent to perceive or suspect or, certainly, to understand. Or, perhaps, simply to help Grandma.

¶¶¶

And what had that obsession really been, and how had it intruded on me, and on my understanding of the world around me? I was seen as having some kind of promise, as being some kind of future. Some of this was likely purely family subconsciousness: I was the second grandchild on Mom's side, and the first grandson; furthermore Joanne's mother was Catholic and not entirely approved by my grandparents.

My birth position, among us grandchildren, was analogous to that of my uncle Charles, and the very name must have reinforced some of a sense of hope. He'd died young, in his late teens I think, of what everyone referred to as "creeping paralysis" on the few occasions they referred to it at all. Mom remembered that it had begun with a loss of sensitivities in the feet, then the legs. When he could no longer walk Gram carried him about; her own eventual crippling was partly the result of her carrying a fully grown man about, my aunts explained to me.

Toward the end, Mom remembered, Charles was completely paralyzed. But he kept a sunny disposition, according to family legend; aunt Dorothy remembers playing checkers with him, when he could only move the pieces by pushing them with a pencil held between his teeth. Not many years later my uncles Clay and David had crossed the Pacific in their turn; of Mom's brothers only Bobby was left at home, and he was never likely to show any promise. Probably dyslexic by today's diagnoses, he was practically illiterate. Dad told me he thought Bobby would never manage in trade school, but Dad helped him learn the rudiments of sheet metalworking.

Dad wasn't really much approved, either: he had ridden into Berkeley, figuratively speaking, on a freight train; he had only a sixth-grade education (and that one suspect); he wasn't much of a churchgoer. The future of the Crane family, Mom's family, didn't seem very promising. And this was important. Education was a serious business on my mother's side of the family. Gramp was a high-school teacher. His father had been a grammar-school teacher. I was probably expected to be, at the least, a college professor. (In fact, Gramp, then nearing his ninetieth birthday, was visibly relieved when I did finally get a job teaching in a college.) True, Mom had dropped out of college to marry Dad, but that could be chalked up to the Depression. Recovery from the Depression and the War would reveal a better world, and children, especially children like me, would make that world.

Mom's two best friends had similarly married and ended their college careers. Edith Duggan — was her mother the Irishwoman Gram visited down near Ashby Street?— had married Will Irwin, a big, slow-footed, goofy-looking, extremely nearsighted man who rose through the ranks of the GallenKamp chain of shoe stores to become some kind of middle-level executive. We visited Edith and Will often; they lived down McKinley Street from us, past the Washington School playground, in a small apartment, when we lived at McKinley and Allston, across from the police station, where I'd been sick with the whooping cough.

Childless at the time, Edith and Will seemed to dote on me. I would look on while the grown-ups played cards, Jim either not yet born, or perhaps parked with Gram, or, on at least one occasion, sleeping in the bathtub, dry of course and cushioned with blankets. And Will, who was truly brilliant, would quiz me on mental arithmetic and the multiplication tables, and talk about astronomy and such, and teach me the moves of the chess pieces, and indulged me in simple games of chess.

Sarah was quite different, dark rather than blonde, willowy and graceful rather than limping like Edith (who had had a minor brush with the then-common Infantile Paralysis). She and her husband Bob Martin lived in a house, not an apartment; and they had a child nearly my age, Anastasia. Bob spoke very quietly and smoked a pipe and wore brown jackets. Sarah used to read to us both, especially A.A. Milne; and Mom and Dad were occasionally given surplus records from the Art Music shop up on Telegraph, where Bob worked. During the war we saw both these couples frequently: card games and conversation were the usual entertainment. Phonograph records had to be attended to every couple of minutes; the radio required concentrated listening; television of course was yet to appear.

Occasionally I was left to spend the night with these friends, I don't know why. Mom and Dad felt it important for me to see how other people lived, I know that; perhaps in addition they had other things to do, best done without me hanging around. I only recall one trip of any distance, when we drove to Pacific Grove to visit great-aunts Gladys and Myrtle.

I remember stopping off at the top of the Santa Cruz Mountains, in a hamlet called Holy City — Dad thought the name was hilarious, and wanted me to look into the curious peepshow dioramas on Biblical themes that were set about like country mailboxes on posts. Was this the trip on which I accidentally opened the car door and nearly fell out, saved by my quick-thinking mother grabbing my leg? But we couldn't have been doing more than twenty-five miles an hour; I doubt I'd have been seriously hurt.

I recall also there was a fellow named Roscoe at my great-aunts' house, and that Dad mentioned that he was wearing tennis shoes with his army uniform because his feet were too big for any standard issue shoe, size fourteen. And I recall another road trip, even further, before Jim was born, when we went up to Silver Lake where Olive and George had a cabin which Dad had helped to build; there we swam and rode horses.

Oklahoma, 1944-45

The ride to Oklahoma was eventful. The Mojave Desert seemed endless, Dad speeding down into the many dips between sand-dunes, then switching off the engine to coast up the other side as far as possible before slipping the clutch to re-start the engine, saving gas. At the Arizona border we had to eat all our apricots, so we pulled into Needles, in the middle of the afternoon, and Mom remarked on the heat, one hundred degrees in the shade. We camped that afternoon in a makeshift tent down by the Colorado River, where we and the car rested a day or two before tackling the fearful climb up toward Flagstaff. At the Arizona border we had to eat all our apricots at once: the inspectors refused to let us bring them in.

I remember looking down on Albuquerque from the rise west of town — an improbable city, small but with some high buildings, on the bank of the Rio Grande, where we camped again a night or two before continuing. Here there was a zoo, of all things, and Mom took me there to point out what exotica she could find, and then we set out again on the slow road east.

We stopped to cool off in a small town in eastern New Mexico, and then drove on for twenty miles before we realized we'd forgotten Butch. After a considerable discussion Mom and Dad decided to return for him: he'd got into a fight with the local dogs — "Indian dogs," Dad or Mom said dismissively — and was pretty badly bitten, but we cleaned him up and started out again, only to have the car break down immediately. "Good thing we lost Butch," Dad said, "otherwise we'd be broke down forty miles out into the prairie with no help in sight."

Finally the trip ended, provisionally, in Guymon, Oklahoma, a railroad town on the panhandle above Amarillo. Here we spent a couple of months, I don't know why — maybe Dad found a job, and God knows we must have been broke. We lived in a house-trailer; I did schoolwork (though it was summer, I think) at the dropleaf table, and Jim sat across from me, learning to read upside down and backward from following in my books. (He didn't learn to read properly until two years later.)

Our trailer was near the tracks, and I waved to the engineers on the switch-engines as they shunted freight cars from one siding to another, and once I was even given a ride in a locomotive, which made Mom furious when she found out. But it was hot and dirty in Guymon, and we soon left, driving across the dusty hills of Oklahoma to the far northeastern corner where Dad had been born thirty-three years before.

There, by the beginning of August, we found Grandma's house, another twostorey white clapboard box of a house but much less genteel than the one on Bancroft Way. For one thing, Grandma's house was really in farm country, on the country side of the unpaved county road that led north to Kansas.

Welch, Oklahoma, was a familiar concept to me. I had seen the name every Saturday, in my father's handwriting on the envelope he addressed to his mother:

> *Mrs. G. H. LaDuke*
> *Welch, Oklahoma*

But I had no idea how unlike Berkeley a backward farm-town Oklahoma would be. Across the road from Grandma's there was a gas station, and beyond it a few houses set far apart, and the community laundry where Mom and Grandma did the wash from time to time, and the school and a park with a baseball diamond, and the business district, a dusty block-long main street, far too wide, with the general store at one end and the jail at the other.

Grandma's house stood at the edge of the prairie stretching out west. There was only one house beyond hers in that direction, a modern one-story one belonging to Mr and Mrs Dobbs. Mr Dobbs was a minister of some sort and rather a scary man; I was warned not to go swimming in his pond on Sundays or he'd give me a thrashing. (And one day I was frightened out of the pond anyway by a swimming snake, and I never swam there again.)

Grandma pastured her milk-cow on Mr. Dobbs's property, and it was often my job to lead Elsie there, or bring her back in the evening, when Dad milked her out in the barn that doubled as a garage. I spent hours in the haymow above the milk parlor and garage, reading I suppose. There was a henhouse nearby where we got our eggs, and a small garden where Grandma raised the vegetables. And there was an old-fashioned cast-iron pump with a curving handle, for Grandma still drew her own water from her well; and there was an outhouse, for there was no indoor plumbing.

In fact one of the reasons we were there in Oklahoma was that Dad wanted to install electrical wiring and plumbing for his mother, now a widow and not getting any younger. She still worked in the local hospital, and Dad worked too; he'd got a job in a synthetic-rubber plant in Miami, the nearest sizable town, where tires were being made for the Army.

Mom stayed home and kept house, as best she could. She was expecting her third child now, and there was that to prepare, knitting and sewing and the like. There was canning to do as well, and Jim and me to look after and, I imagine, protect from our rougher cousins.

It was hard to sort out the near relatives from those more distant. Uncle Alvie and Aunt Fay, as Mom taught me to call Flora Mae, were easy to place, but they lived up in Chetopa Kansas and we didn't see them too often. The dusty road alongside Grandma's house led straight there, making one dog-leg to avoid some recalcitrant citizen's fields, then jumping up nearly a foot to meet the paved Kansas road.

Along the way we more often took a side road off east to

Great-Grandma's farm. This seemed exotic to me, somehow; her big old farmhouse was shaded by big trees, and its sloping farmyard led down to a creek. Great-Grandma didn't even even have a pump; she drew her water from a dug well, in a bucket at the end of a rope. She smoked a corncob pipe, and had no teeth that I could see, and had recently taught herself to read, Dad told me proudly; and indeed when we visited she was often sitting in her spindly wooden rockingchair with her pipe clamped somehow in her mouth, reading her Bible, for the women on Dad's side of the family were as religious as they were on Mom's side, and maybe more devout.

There were relatives more distant, cousins of Dad's I suppose, and their children, close to my age, a rough-and-tumble lot who liked wrestling and teasing and who scared me a little. And there were others, cousins who'd gone off to war, and one, Ivan was his improbable name, who stayed with us in Grandma's house at Christmastime, on furlough I suppose from recruitment camp, as he wasn't much more than eighteen years old.

I was in the fifth grade now, because the Oklahoma schools wouldn't keep me on a mid-year course, and Mom had argued them into letting me skip the second half of the fourth grade rather than start it over. She armed herself with a letter of urgent recommendation from a Berkeley psychology professor who'd been studying me there, for she'd enrolled me in some kind of study that tracked kids over a number of years, administering frequent intelligence tests and observing us in occasional interviews. This seems odd, now, sixty years later; but at the time there was a vogue for social engineering, for using science to improve not only the world but also its inhabitants. I can't imagine what the Welch school administration would have thought of this, but they probably didn't want any further arguments with Mom, and having just turned nine years old I was set down in the fifth grade, of which I recall precisely nothing.

Instead I recall climbing around among the rafters of the

community wash-house, where I stuck my curious finger into an empty light-socket and got a shock; I recall daring a cousin to lick the frozen pump-handle, and getting a licking myself after Grandma thawed his tongue off the cast-iron with body-temperature water from the teakettle; I recall baths in the galvanized-iron washtub on Saturday nights, the tub set in the middle of the kitchen floor; and I recall "dancing" on my hands and knees, like a demented ballet horse, to the overtures to *Countess Maritza* and *The Gypsy Baron* and *The Student Prince*, all in an album of shellac 78-rpm records Mom had brought with us all the way from Berkeley.

And I recall vividly that my brother John was born the following spring, April 13, 1945, the day after Franklin Roosevelt died. There had been a terrible storm that night. There had been a lot of bad weather that year: we'd been scared more than once into the storm-cellar, where Grandma kept the jars of fruit she canned. There'd been snowstorms now and then, and lots of electrical storms, when I dove under the bed, because Grandma said lightning wouldn't penetrate the feather mattresses; and one morning we looked down from our bedroom window to see a meandering brown trail burned into the lawn, left by a ball of lightning that had wandered across the grass in the night.

But the storm of the night of April 12 was the worst of all, with Mom crying, and Grandma comforting her, and Dad listening to the crackling radio and finally reporting that the President had died.

"Good," Mom said; she'd never approved of Franklin D. Roosevelt; and they bundled into the car and drove to Miami where John was born.

And then before long Berlin had fallen, and Grandma's wiring and plumbing was finished, and we drove north, our family of five, to spend the summer of 1945 in another house-trailer, parked unwisely under a cottonwood tree in Topeka, Kansas.

This was something of an idyll, as I think about it — a warm drowsy summer that left me pretty well to myself, with no school, no bullies, no incomprehensible distant relatives. I played outside among the cottonwoods, looking out from them down on the nearby Topeka, its capitol dome glistening in the sun, or I sat reading at the dropleaf table, and Jim, having just turned five years old, sat across from me, still reading upside down and backward from following in my books.

Our trailer was pretty shabby, though, and Dad decided to paint it, probably to ready it for sale, to prepare for our return to California. I don't recall ever hearing any news about the war, the Pacific campaign, or the bombing of Hiroshima and Nagasaki, but this was August, 1945, the European campaign was over, and one way or another the war was clearly soon to end altogether.

So we painted the house trailer, a snappy two-tone job, silver above, jet black below; and that night a wind came up and the cottonwoods lost all their fuzz, and we woke up next morning living in what looked like a huge bale of cotton, fresh paint oddly showing through in patches. Dad chanted his long familiar string of obscenities; Mom bit her lip; Jim and I chuckled.

And then Mom and Jim and the baby and I went back to Berkeley on the Greyhound bus, another trip of which I remember nothing whatever, to spend a week or so with Gramp and Gram in the house they had recently moved to, low in the Berkeley hills north of campus, on Glen Avenue, across the street from a delightful wasteland of blackberries and poisonoak, bisected by a creek and waterfalls. Aunt Dorothy was staying there, waiting for Uncle Lester to return from the war: she occupied the large mezzanine bedroom, where she spent hours sprawled on her bed in the daytime, it seemed to me, listening to records. She had an up-to-date Philco record player; you slid the records into a slot and the machine magically centered it and played it, and then stuck it back out so you could turn it over and repeat the process for the other side. George

Gershwin's *Rhapsody in Blue* was a favorite of hers; I remember the drawing on the cover, an elevated train leaning into the night, and I remember the sound of the opening of the piece, so different from *Countess Maritza* and *The Gypsy Baron*.

And then, in September, Dad arrived, still driving the Ford station wagon, and we settled in completely new surroundings, isolated it seemed to me in the country in Sonoma county, seven miles south of Sebastopol.

with my brother Jim, Mom with John on her lap,
in the doorway at "The Ranch," fall of 1945

2: "The Ranch,"1945-1948

IT'S ONE OF THE MANY FACTS now permanently lost to me: how we came to settle there. There was a book on our shelves, *Five Acres and Independence*, that may have had something to do with this. Or it may have been *The Egg and I,* another book extolling life in the country. Mr. Jensen's paradise in Castro Valley, and our short stay in Lafayette, were precursors. Clearly Dad had a lot to do with this decision: I'm sure he was never really at home in Berkeley: he got along fine with Bob and Sarah, Edith and Will, but less well with Gramp and Gram, and he had some goodnatured contempt for Mom's odd lot of brothers and sisters, sensing perhaps the various degrees of variance between the bohemian lives they'd led as young adults and the postures they adopted with their conservative church-going parents.

The Oklahoma experience must have brought his position home to him, as it were: he was no longer an Okie, too traveled, too aware of the multiplicities of experiences of Carmel and Berkeley to take a permanent place in Welch or Miami. But he knew he wasn't really a city boy, either: his accent and his outlook set him apart, in an intellectual community; and his eyes were used to seeing farther than down the street.

Nor do I know who found the place we settled on: again, perhaps, great-uncle Percy, or uncle Dave, both of whom had settled for the time being in Sonoma county. The only memory I have of these proceedings was a trip I made alone with Dad from Berkeley up to the country: we were on the Richmond-San Rafael ferry, the bridge not yet having been built, and we were sitting on the long bench under an overhang on the top deck — Dad always liked harsh weather, I think — and somehow his wallet escaped his pocket, and we didn't notice until we saw it slide slowly but inexorably across the wet deck, under the steel-mesh barrier under the guard rail, and into the gray-green San Francisco Bay. It was one of those moments when Dad's face could register simultaneous disbelief, hurt, a little bit of rage, and resignation. He had an immensely complex emotional life.

What to call the broken-down property we inhabited now? Dad always called it The Ranch, and so do my brothers, but that always seemed far too grand to me. It wasn't really a Farm, because we never sold any product from it that I know of, apart from an experimental business in cream from our two cows. I have always thought of this property as Blank Road, the road our mailbox stood on, seven-tenths of a mile from our house.

I had just turned ten years old when we moved there. My first decade had been spent in Berkeley, first among Depression-era intellectuals and eccentric young aunts and uncles and my comforting, warm grandmother, interrupted by wartime Richmond and capped by the dislocating , disturbing year in Oklahoma and Kansas. The next seven years would be spent on this hardscrabble "farm," again punctuated by an interruption a year and a half long in Berkeley; and this counterpoise of town and country, society and isolation, comfort and privation marked me for years to come.

What were the privations? Well, for one thing, electricity and telephone and hot water and the like. Mom and Dad had bought two adjacent properties, neither closer than three-quarters of a mile to the nearest paved road. One, the Ten Acre as we called it (I'm sure A.A. Milne's *Winnie the Pooh* influenced that appellation), had no building or improvement of any kind: it was a steep hillside descending from a row of old cypresses marking the fenceline, dropping toward a gully this side of which stood a eucalyptus woodlot that would provide our heat and cooking fuel for the next ten years.

The other property was seventeen acres, half of it cleared, half — beyond a more serious extension of that same gully — in mixed woodland of scrub oak and madrone and poisonoak.

As we found the place there were three buildings. At the bottom of a hill there was a run-down horse barn under a huge pine tree, fragrant with ancient leather tack and long-gone alfalfa and the pungent, enticing fragrance of old horse-manure and -sweat. A hundred yards or so up a driveway from the barn stood a threestorey tankhouse of the familiar type: four huge redwood timbers at the corners, gradually tapering up from ground to platform, with a big redwood water tank at the top. And, at its foot, our house.

This was a decrepit thing, a two-room cabin with a kitchen on the east, a livingroom on the west. A sort of lean-to attachment ran along the north side, overlooking the remains of an ornamental flower garden; this provided a bedroom for Jim and me on the east, another for Mom and Dad and the baby on the west, with a tiny bathroom between.

We lived so for the first year, at first trying to make do with the 32-volt DC electrical system that had come with the place: a gas-driven generator and a fascinating array of square glass batteries, housed in a little shed at the foot of the water tank. But this quickly proved too troublesome: one had to continually adjust the water-acid mixture in the batteries, correcting the balance of little red, yellow, and green balls in mysterious windows of the batteries, starting and stopping the engine, cleaning its spark plug, all for an amount of undependable electricity insufficient in any case for much beyond a couple of dim light bulbs.

There was a kerosene cook-stove with a built-in trash burner, and another kerosene heating stove that barely got us through the first winter. I don't recall any refrigeration in the kitchen — that first winter it would hardly have been necessary. We did have running water, thanks to the tankhouse, but it was cold, and hard, and stained the bathtub and toilet with rust.

Beyond these inconveniences, though, lay the real problem soon to appear: after the first serious rains, usually in late November or early December, our long dirt road was unusable. There would be a week or so when we'd continue to try to use it, and we would frequently have to haul the car out of the mud, levering it up with a long eucalyptus pole, throwing stuff under the tires, or even simply muscling it to one side of whatever pit it had sunk into. But sooner or later it would become necessary to leave the car out near the paved road and carry all our provisions home — sacks of potatoes and onions, heavier sacks of feed for the cows and pigs and chickens.

The original idea had been to sustain ourselves on this place, but Dad worked in town. At first he worked fairly nearby, in a factory that manufactured stoves of some kind — it may have been here that he was able to salvage various experiments at heating our cabin. Later, either to improve the paycheck or to escape an unpleasant work environment, he took one job or another further away, in Santa Rosa, fifteen miles distant, a long drive in those days, and on uncertain roads in the winter.

This routine left only the weekends to try to improve the property, but the following spring we set to it. Dad threw a symmetrical lean-to up against the south side of the cabin, with a small bedroom just for me at the west end, against the small cherry orchard, and a new kitchen and dining-room looking south across Mom's strawberry patch toward the blackberry vines she'd planted. On the covered porch of this new wing stood an icebox, for the hot summer was coming.

There was still no electricity, but the newly installed wood-burning cookstove had a coil of pipes next to the firebox, and a small amount of lukewarm water was now often available on tap, though we still boiled water in pots and pans for the very occasional baths. The curtain wall between the two original rooms came down, and we had more light and air in the living room that resulted. Here there was another wood-burning stove for heat, made not of cast iron but of some kind of sheet steel.

We entertained ourselves in this room in the evenings, sitting in furniture Dad had made out of automobile seats, along with the remnants of our fine city households — a maple dining set, and a platform rocker, the stuffing protruding here and there from tears in its loose-weave upholstery cloth.

Mom sat on one side of the stove, knitting or mending; Dad on the other, reading or cleaning something. Once it was his .22 rifle, and when Mom automatically emptied the ashtray into the stove there followed a short time later two or three little explosions, for Dad had set aside the bullets from the rifle. They went through the sheet iron side of the stove, but no one was hit. Dad thought this very funny (and so did I), but scolded Mom for not looking at the ashtray. Mom was angry and called him a fool. I still have the habit of looking twice at things I put in the stove, and always look into the oven before turning it on.

There was a lamp that burned white gasoline, a very bright lamp that made it possible for us to read, and in the evenings we took turns, Mom, Dad, and I, reading aloud from various wartime novels then still popular — I still remember *The Moon is Down*, and *Mrs. Miniver*, and *The Corn is Green*. Dad smoked Prince Albert tobacco in his corncob pipe, and Mom smoked her Dominos and, later, Wings, cheap brands both.

There was an upright piano — I have no idea where it came from, but I remember it being out of tune and missing a number of ivories. Mom sat at it very occasionally; I more often, until in a year or so it slowly settled into such decline it was no longer playable.

But these hours were short, and soon I would go to bed. My bed was curiously high, I suppose with some sort of closet below it, and I slept a foot or so below the ceiling, conveniently raised just over my head by a boxed-in skylight Dad had made of an old window. Through it I could see my lovely night sky, and track the constellations that had fascinated me for years, since I'd been given a book about them and the Greek myths they stood for; and I could listen to the owls. On the walls there were two reproductions: Raphael's *Madonna and Child* and Gilbert Stuart's unfinished portrait of George Washington. I suppose these were meant to give me, by some magical optical osmosis, a kind of awareness of God and Country: but the only effect I remember from them is a fondness for the Madonna's blue and the discomfort of Washington's challenging eye, following me wherever I went in my room.

Who were my companions in those months? I had one friend at school, Kent: he lived in a house a mile or so to the east of our place, and our paths to school coincided only in their last mile or so, but we conversed and traded sandwiches (when mine were edible) and generally maintained our elite shyness and disdain for physicality against the other boys, who played football and baseball and delighted in threatening us.

It could have been worse: there were misfits even more outlandish than us, a very tall, skinny, stupid, redheaded boy and his oddly short, fat, but equally stupid sister. Kent tormented them, verbally and intellectually, as he and I were tormented physically by the others. Miss Thompson looked on, trying to teach us to take comfort in books and knowledge, but facilities were few, and before long I'd read through most of the books in the small bookcase that served as school library — chiefly the work of Albert Payson Terhune.

At lunchtime we'd occasionally venture, Kent and I, to the little general store across the street from school, where we could buy an ice-cream cone for a nickel, and ice milk for only three cents. But I didn't often have the three cents. When we returned from Oklahoma to Berkeley I had for some reason been given a fairly thorough physical exam, the day after consuming an enormous amount of candy provided by always solicitous Gram, and my blood sugar level tested quite high. They suspected an incipient diabetes, and for years after I was denied candy: to ensure I didn't cheat, I was given very little pocket money — not that there was much to spare in our family in any case.

Beyond the general store Hessel Road wound up and over a hill, Fat Lady Hill we called it for the woman who lived near its top; and beyond the hill it dropped and ran on straight for a mile or so north to the highway that led to Sebastopol. I rarely strayed to that side of the hill, though one Hallowe'en there was a party in an apple-drying shed on a farm out there. The girl who lived there, Eileen, was rude and brassy, I always thought, but she invited me and, I think, Jim, and I went, unwillingly, and endured the bobbing for apples and the walk through a chamber of horrors, pitch-black, with slimy apple-peeling strips hanging down from the ceiling to brush our faces as we groped our way through.

Hessel was a community of sorts, with the school, the store, a cluster of houses; and it had a community church. I attended it for a few weeks, I suppose because Mom thought I should be exposed to Christianity as a prevalent component of the American culture. I didn't enjoy it, and resisted the memorization of Scripture and the suspect moralizing, which already seemed hypocritical to me. Told I'd win a prize for memorizing a verse from the New Testament, I memorized John 11:35, "Jesus wept," and was grudgingly awarded a copy of the Bible; I still have it, the only one I've ever owned. When the weather got bad I stopped attending, rather than walk the six miles there and back in the rain.

There were few visitors to our new home. There must have been a certain amount of turmoil back in Berkeley, with sons-in-law returning from the War, Uncle Clay recovering from his four years' imprisonment in the Philippines, and the general return to peacetime economy and business. Gramp and Gram did drive up at least once, in their old Hudson, running better now there was gasoline for it rather than the paint thinner Gramp had burned during the War. Bob and Sarah came up at least once; it made an impression on me that Mom had told Dad to get a bottle of sherry, something I'd never heard of before, because it was something Sarah particularly liked.

I think Edith and Will were up once or twice, with their new little girl Gene; and perhaps Edith's sister June and her brother Curt came up as well, for Mom kept up her friendship with them throughout. But Blank Road was a long way from Berkeley in those days: the highway was nothing but a two-lane road; there were long waits for the ferry; cars were slow and gas still expensive.

I spent my days either at Eucalyptus School or, on weekends and in summer, at chores, or reading, or daydreaming. I was now in sixth grade, though only just turned ten. Eucalyptus School was a two-room affair then, two large rooms in a white shiplap building surmounted by the usual bell-cupola. The little kids, kindergarten through fifth grade, were in one room; our room was for sixth, seventh, and eighth grade, perhaps four rows of six or seven desks, with Miss Thompson's desk behind, and the blackboard in front, and a piano on one side, along with the small bookcase for recreational reading.

I walked to school. It was about three miles there, three miles back, and this gave me two hours' exercise, wonderful in good weather when I could ramble across shortcuts that inevitably lengthened the walk home but quite unpleasant on rainy days when between the mud and the rain I'd arrive at either end of my commute soaked and cold and, in the morning, the object of some derision for my schoolmates.

By now I was old enough to begin forming some opinion of them as individuals, with lives of their own apart from (indeed very different from) mine, not simply as other human animals, present when I was present, otherwise with no independent existence. The beginning of consciousness is perhaps in the development of this kind of awareness, that there is an outside world apart from one's own home and immediate family, and that it has an existence of its own and can do very well without you. And from this it follows that one is free to develop one's own way of existing, which can very well differ completely from the other.

So I would hurry to school in the morning, freely swinging my schoolbooks and lunchbag in good weather, clutching them against me under my slicker on rainy days; and spend the day mostly reading but occasionally listening in on the lessons the seventh- and eighth-graders were getting, if they offered something I hadn't already picked up somewhere on my own; and enjoying the music lessons when we all read new songs from the blackboard or the music textbook, singing in harmony, even, songs like "The Old Oaken Bucket" and "In The Gloaming" and "Old Folks at Home" and "Old Dog Tray." Once a week our entire room listened to the *Standard School Hour*, a radio program that featured light classical music often performed by the Longines Symphonette — a name that seemed exotic and distant — or arias and duets sung by matinee idols like John Charles Thomas and Lily Pons., or sometimes the folk-singers Josef Marais and Miranda, bringing the exotic world of South Africa into our two-room country school.

At recess and during the lunch hour we were made to play games on the dirt playfield: the bigger boys played softball, practicing for occasional outings, somehow, to neighboring grammar schools for special games. I had no aptitude, it seemed, and was invariably chosen last, if at all, when the teams were selected. This suited me; I was mistrustful and preferred to be left alone, or with one or two other similarly unsocietized misfits. We read, or played mumbletypeg if the teacher wasn't looking, or Andy-Over, with a basketball, across the school's pumphouse.

At lunchtime I would have my sandwiches: peanut butter and honey, one of them, and fried-egg. But the honey was unpleasant, full of bits of honeybees, for Mom tended the hives better than she sieved the honey she collected. And the egg was cold, hard, and greasy. And the bread was embarrassing more often than not: impossibly full of holes when the yeast was fresh; passable for a week or two when it was just right; impossibly dense and unchewable when the yeast was at the end of its life, and Mom hadn't yet prepared a new pot of it.

The walk home, in pleasant weather, was the best part of routine in those days, unless I got into a fight on the first part of it, which took me past widely separated houses where other boys lived. Once past the first mile, when I'd reached Blank Road and turned west uphill toward our mailbox, I was on my own, past the Portuguese house, as we called it, because its inhabitants kept goats, and were said to live on cheese and wild mushrooms, and then to the mailbox where I gathered the mail, and then down our own road, along the fragrant huge blue gums, and past the enticing willow wood where the blackberries blossomed late in the spring, and then between a neighbor's pasture and the creek with its scrub forest, where the trilliums bloomed unforgettably in the early spring; and then, as slowly as possible, across the cattle-guard that marked the nearness of our own place, and across the mud-bog at the bottom of our hill, and past the horse barn and thus home to chores.

That last mile of the walk was often a reverie. I smelled the eucalyptus acorns and leaves and bark, each with its distinctive fragrance; and looked for special stones, quartz or obsidian or marbled red-and-whites; and wandered along the cowpaths in the pasture belonging to The Dairy, as we called it, whose house and barns stood at the end of Hessel Road where it met Blank Road after passing the mysterious Apple Drier and the Pencil Factory on its railroad siding and, below and just this side the Pencil Factory, the amazing mimosa tree, huge and dark but decked with lacy light-green foliage and, marking the end of spring, fabulous displays of yellow blossoms whose perfume stayed with me for several minutes after walking past it.

Toward the end of the walk came the best part, The Oaks, sparsely scattered and intermixed with delicious cool madrones with glorious Indian-red trunks revealed by the peeling papery bark. Here the scrubby trunks and low foliage resulted in a gentle, dappled light; the alternating light and shade was hypnotizing, and the fragrance of the wet clay banks of the creek, the mossy banks and stones among which I was still young enough to think fairies might live, and the sound of the breeze, of frogs and insects all conjured a sensuous delight that has ever since accompanied country landscape. Occasionally there would be surprising wildlife: a weasel or a squirrel, a startled jackrabbit in the fields, the sharp caw of a crow or the gentler warble of a meadowlark; or I would glimpse a deer or two frozen attentively among the oaks, and fantasize God, whatever God there was, as a white deer, mysteriously majestic and fully engaged with the beauty and the balance of this Nature, teeming with detail and equally pleasant, overwhelmingly pleasant to eye and nose and ear, and soft and gentle to the touch.

And then I'd be home. My chores centered on firewood and the animals; gardening seemed to be a woman's province. We relied mostly on the eucalyptus grove for our firewood, and at first we depended on our own muscles for the power. This must have been good for me; I can't remember ever being sick or sore during those years, apart from one bout with what Mom always called "stomach flu," probably the result of our kitchen facilities rather than anything spread by human society at school.

We used a two-man saw, my father and I, to cut the felled trees into chunks; and double-bit axes, both of us, to split those into stovewood. Eucalyptus has a number of unfortunate properties, and one is that it saws most easily when it is dry, but is possible to split only when it is green. This taught me early the stubbornness of Nature when assaulted by human demand; it also taught me Dad's stubbornness, and swelled my vocabulary.

Before long we gave up on the two-man saw and converted to petroleum power. Dad rigged up a good-sized table that could pivot into a huge rusty circular sawblade mounted at the end of a mandrel; I can't imagine where he found the parts. This was powered via a long canvas belt by one of the rear wheels of our car, jacked up for the occasion. We'd begin by lifting that wheel off the ground, using a long eucalyptus pole as a lever and a chunk of firewood as fulcrum, and set another chunk under the rear axle; then we'd stretch the belt around the tire.

This was frustrating work, as the belt would immediately slip off the tire unless the car and sawtable were perfectly aligned. One of my duties was to keep this from happening, by holding a eucalyptus pole against the edge of the belt, the other end of the pole thrust into the ground. Eventually, though, to my sorrow, things would be in order, and the terrifying work would begin, sawdust and chips flying, exhaust and the smell of powdering rubber-tire filling the air. I think it was the noise that was most hateful: the steady noise of the car engine; the whirring, occasionally flapping sound of the belt; the windy muffled roar of the sawteeth when not engaged in firewood, and the harsher whine when they bit into the dry eucalyptus Dad favored for this operation. And, of course, Dad's comments when the belt slipped, for often enough the firewood would simply stop the buzzsaw, and the tire would spin uselessly inside the now-stationary belt, quickly heating up enough to fill our nostrils, plugged though they were with sawdust, with the sharp smell of burning rubber.

At one point we gave up on all this and began using the neighbor's saw. Mr. Cavanaugh was a mysterious old man who appeared only on occasional weekends and perhaps for a week at a time in the summer. His house was only a hundred yards or so from ours, but out of sight beyond our cherry orchard and a blackberry-and-poisonoak-infested gully and a thick copse of oak and madrone. It was an ancient twostorey house, quite neglected and rarely occupied, and on our side of the gully, accessible from his house via a ramshackle bridge, there was a small barn and carriage-house.

I remember seeing Mr. Cavanaugh only twice, once in his Petaluma house, a mansion to my eye, beautifully furnished and paneled, for he had apparently made his money in the lumber business, and had made his home a showplace. (It has since been turned into a bed-and-breakfast.) The other time was at his country property, when I saw him, old man that he was, pruning his apple trees from the top of a stepladder set on a buckboard: an old horse was standing in the slack traces, ready to draw the apparatus patiently to the next tree.

Between his house and the bridge to his barn there stood an ancient sawtable apparatus, powered by a one-cylinder gas engine with an enormous flywheel. You started this engine by grabbing the rim of the flywheel and pulling it toward you with a sudden jerk. If the engine were properly primed with gasoline it would spring to life, half the time clockwise, the other half in the other direction — in which case you'd stop the engine and start all over, hoping for the best. We carried our poles of dry eucalyptus here on a trailer pulled by the trusty Ford, and sawed them into firewood, and then loaded it all back up again for the trip back.

Sometimes, too, when the wind hadn't blown for days, we'd fill jugs of water from Mr. Cavanaugh's spring-fed tank. Our own water supply depended on wind; the well was deep, too deep for a hand-pump, or I'm sure Dad would have converted to one, out of nostalgia perhaps, or just plain cussedness, as Mom was fond of saying. I loved the sound of our windmill, which creaked when turning slow and hummed when faster; and the steady pulse of the pump itself, the squared wooden shaft bowing slightly when it bottomed out, and stretched on the pull stroke; and the gurgle of the water as it lifted into the big two-inch galvanized pipe that rose at a steep angle to the top of the water tower, a long prop supporting it at the half-way point — I think the constant awareness of this apparatus was fundamental to my developing sense of geometry and proportion.

The tankhouse itself was filling up with all sorts of things. Over the years Dad built a staircase on one side, the side nearest the house and strawberry bed, and floored the second level of the tower, for yet more storage. There were shelves for the jars of fruit Mom put up most summers; and on the first floor of the tankhouse, dark and dank and spiderwebby, there were a couple of stoneware jars, covered with chipped crockery plates, filled with fermenting sauerkraut.

Mom made jam, too, of course, and bread, as I've already noted, with her own little pot of yeast that stood on the windowsill; and, a few years later on, after the kitchen had been moved yet again, she made cottage cheese. But that was years later, when I was in high school. In these first two years the kitchen was too small for any but the most necessary work. The sloping ceiling was quite low, barely clearing Dad's head when he stood — so when the pressure cooker exploded one day, and its lid split into two halves and went flying to the ceiling, one part actually lodging in it, and the two half-moon marks were left for us to marvel at for months, and shake our heads at what would have happened if Mom had been leaning over the pot at that moment, you can see that the effect wasn't quite as dramatic as it sounds to someone whose kitchen ceiling is up where it should be, eight or nine feet above the floor.

Our table was attached at one side to the wall, just under a series of sliding glass windows, with Dad at the far end, and Mom at the stove end, and Jim and me and John in his high chair along the side. At breakfast on weekends we'd linger over pancakes, putting off the firewood expedition, and in the spring Dad would sometimes take down the .22 rifle that hung over the kitchen windows, and I'd quietly slide one of them open, and he'd take shots at a solitary quail sentinel posted atop a stake among the blackberry bushes, where the coveys of quail liked to feed in the early morning. Now and then he'd actually hit one, in spite of his one weak eye, and after a bit another would fly up to replace it, and he'd peg away at that one; and sometimes we had enough for next day's breakfast.

The clothesline was strung out near the windmill, in a kind of corridor-yard that led to the pigsty and milk-barn beyond. The grass grew tall in this yard, and there were a couple of geese that sometimes had their run, and would come up behind and bite when you reached up to unpin the wash that had been flapping in the afternoon breeze. And beyond was a low jerry-built cabin that had come with the place, with an unglazed window and a plank floor, a door on leather-strap hinges for access from the house side, and two or three large vats made from oil drums cut in half. In these vats we poured milk and water and occasional kitchen scraps, thickening the result with rolled barley we bought at the feed store; and one of my jobs was to tend this disgusting but enticingly scented slop, and ladle it out into buckets that I then carried, one in each hand, out to the pigsty.

The other side of this building was where Dad milked the cows. Here there was no floor but the bare dirt, packed by the cows and covered with straw. We had two cows that I remember. Daisy was my favorite, a small Jersey with a darker blaze on her muzzle and incredibly deep and gentle eyes; but I liked Goldie too, half Jersey and half Guernsey, taller, and mottled in a redder brown (hence her name) and white instead of the dark and darker browns of the Jersey.

I loved these cows and hated the bad days when Dad was completely out of temper. Sometimes a cow would accidentally flick her tail into his face, and he'd jump up from the one-legged stool he used, simply a short piece of two-by-four nailed crosswise to the end of another, and snatch it up and begin clubbing her with it: at such moments I'd run away sometimes, crying, compounding the issue of course, and Mom would bite her lip and try somehow to reassure me, and I'd hear recriminations later that night issuing from the mysterious room in which they slept and argued.

We sold the cream from this milk, and drank some of what remained, and poured the rest into the pig slops. I separated the cream from its milk, turning the crank of a DeLaval separator; and since I can remember that it was at its proper speed when I'd cranked it up to a steady F-sharp I know that this must have been years later, when I was in high school and studying music and had such information in mind. In the first years we perhaps had only one cow, and Mom let the cream rise of its own accord, and skimmed it off to make our butter, churning it in a half-gallon jar with an eggbeater-like apparatus attached to its lid.

The milk was delicious, even the skim milk with flecks of rubbery cream floating in it, but I could never develop a taste for the buttermilk, which in any case was reserved for Dad. There was plenty of milk to go around, at least in my memory, though there must have been times when Daisy went dry, and we had to buy our milk at the store. The eggs were delicious, too, though I was troubled by their dirty shells, with bits of straw frequently stuck to them, and now and then by flecks of blood in the yolks. We had chickens and ducks as well as the geese, and these too were my responsibility; I scattered the chicken-scratch in the chickenyard, and filled the ducks' feeders with mash; and while I was disgusted with the state of the duckyard — there's nothing dirtier than a flock of imprisoned ducks — I was enthralled with the iridescent green heads of the Mallard drakes, and the marvelous chevrons at their shoulders, and even the melody, complacent and satisfied, of their quacking.

I was equally entranced with the beautifully speckled coats of the Guinea fowl who had free run of the yard, like the geese, and who surprised us sometimes in the spring with unsuspected clutches of chicks, suddenly emerging peeping and skittering among the grasses; and then Mom would make little cages of chicken-wire to protect her seedlings from them, and let them go scratching about the vegetable garden, keeping down the insect population.

What I did not like was the butchering. Mom didn't either, and left it all to Dad, who seemed to delight in it. The rabbits were the worst of all: Dad simply put his foot on the head of the terrified animal, and pulled on the hindquarters, and off came the head with a shriek. Then he pulled the pelt off the carcass as you'd pull your sweater over your head, and it would be my job to stretch it on a frame made of a sturdy wire coathanger and hang it, first in the sun, later when dry in the tankhouse, and when we had a few of them they'd be taken to town one day and sold, I don't know where.

And the rabbit would of course be eaten. To this day I am not fond of rabbit; its flesh is sweet and tightly packed, and roasted whole it looks unfortunately anatomical. Of course the same is true of suckling pig, and I don't mind eating that at all — perhaps because after slaughtering a pig we were so angry with the beast that its end seemed perfectly justified. But rabbits always seemed benighted and defenseless. I had to care for them at first, but apparently did it badly enough that Mom took over their care and feeding — perhaps from the terrible morning when I discovered, on going out to feed and water them in their hutches, a good-sized snake devouring a batch of just-born kittens. I shouted, and Mom came running, and caught up an axe and dispatched the snake.

The rabbit hutches stood between the henhouse and the duckyard, behind a small vegetable patch of some kind. The rabbits were big and white — New Zealand Whites, I believe — with disgustingly yellowed feet from standing in their own droppings: no matter how often we cleaned, these droppings seemed to pile up in some inaccessible corner, and that of course was where they preferred to spend their cowering hours. Now and then Dad would put a buck in the doe's cages, and there'd be a quick frenzy, and then the buck would fall over exhausted on its side and be taken up and restored to his own cage. This was my sex education, and it did little to encourage further interest for a number of years.

I liked the pigs, those early years, up until the day came that we butchered one. They lived in a muddy pen, with a low hut, hardly bigger than they, in which to take refuge on hot sunny days; and they ate their slops from a trough Dad had made by cutting one side off a long rather narrow old-fashioned hot-water tank. They wore rings in their noses; I had to help ring the piglets, holding them down while Dad clamped the sharp-ended open rings through the cartilage of their noses. This was to keep them from rooting and especially from digging their way under their fence: but it did not always work, and there were times they'd get out, and we'd have to go looking for them, and corner them up against a building somewhere and grab them. On such occasions Dad might fashion a lasso and finally loop it around a neck or an ankle: this always made me think him an exotic cowboy type, and probably satisfied his hankerings for such a life, at least for a little while.

I don't recall trips into town during those first couple of years. There were times Mom and Dad would drive in, probably on Saturdays to do some kind of shopping, and I'd be left home with my brothers. These were special days when we could do forbidden things, like bounce on the furniture and play don't-touch-the-floor, jumping from couch to chair and back; or we would explore our parents' bedroom, or the upper reaches of the tankhouse. Otherwise we worked outside. That first year we fenced the Ten Acres, and Dad patiently taught me that you always need one more post than you think, unless the fence completely encloses a field. He dug the postholes with a clamshell digger, the sort my son now calls idiot sticks, and I would be fascinated and so, I think, would he, at the things that would turn up in the excavated dirt, bits of shiny black obsidian, rusty nails, bits of flint sometimes but never an arrowhead.

This fencing job took us to a magical place at one corner of the Ten Acres, where a rutted dirt road led down from our place along a fenceline of eucalyptus trees to a paved road, Orchard Station Road, which remained beyond my world until quite later on. At this corner there must have been a farmhouse or a squatter's cabin many years earlier, because there were a few rosebushes gone wild, and Japanese Lanterns (they'd been re-named Chinese Lanterns only a few years earlier, during the War), and a couple of ancient scrappy apple trees. The fenceline behind this corner was the eastern boundary of our place, and was planted in very old cypresses, fenceline cypresses we always called them, there were many such fencelines in southwestern Sonoma county; and their branches were so horizontal, so close-set, and started so low to the ground that one day our dog Butch, quite recovered from his squabble a couple of years earlier with the Indian dogs, chased a cat across the pasture and right up into the tree, and climbed ladder-style a good six or eight feet up before he realized what he was doing, and yelped until I was able to haul him back down again.

For a couple of years we raised hay on the steep slope of the Ten Acres. We plowed it, I don't know how; and then Mom and Dad and I walked the hillside scattering the seed, one year by hand, taking seed by the handful from apron pockets and scattering it with rhythmic sweeping gestures from our opened fists, the next year with store-bought hand-cranked hoppers of some kind, which Mom thought more consistent in the resulting pattern, and Dad resisted as an unnecessarily modernized refinement.

We mowed the hay one year with scythes, and the next with a sicklebar, a frightening machine with triangular plates of razor-sharp steel which slid back and forth along a long flat bar. Dad had borrowed this apparatus from someone, and he strode ahead or beside it somehow, driving the mule, and it was my job to walk behind and warn him if he was about to cut into an uneven part of ground; and Butch, who was following along, somehow fell into the sicklebar and lost a good patch of skin from his side, which filled me with terror and Dad with scorn and anger, because it cost us the rest of the day and a trip to the veterinarian.

There had been another serious injury, potentially much more serious: one day when walking home from school, when a number of the other boys were breaking into the then-inactive pencil factory and raising hell, I noticed smoke coming out of the disused apple drier. Investigating with another boy I found a pile of bright yellow sulfur from which the acrid smoke was rising, a pool of blue fire at its base. He ran to alert someone and I tried to stamp the fire out, not realizing how dangerous and slippery the burning sulfur was. I slipped and fell into the fire, stopping myself with my left forearm and my right hand.

My left shirtsleeve began to smolder as I ran home, and by the time I got to the Portuguese house I could go no further. I pounded on the door and the Portuguese wife, who I'd never seen before, let me in, tore off my shirt, smeared my arm with butter and wrapped it in gauze, then phoned the doctor in Sebastopol. We of course did not have a telephone and I don't know how Mom heard about all this. I spent a week or so in Palm Drive Hospital, where Doctor Sharrocks treated me with penicillin and grafted bits of skin taken from my thigh to cover the alarming stretch of burned skin on my arm: these were techniques he'd learned during the recent war, and without them I'd probably have been crippled or worse.

There were happier times, too, of course. There was a wonderful week or so when the cherries were ripe: we had three huge Bing trees, and four or five Royal Annes, and a couple of Black Tartarians; and when they were ripe I'd spend an hour or so in the branches, eating cherries and reading; and then we'd pick the cherries, and Mom would can them, marking the lids with NP to signify that they had No Pits, or some years that they were Not Pitted, we never remembered which until the jar was opened and the answer was clear.

She canned pears, too, though I think not from our own trees; I don't recall any pear trees. These were Bartlett pears, and they canned nicely, peeled and halved, with cinnamon red-hot candies added to some jars, and a leaf or two of mint and some green food coloring to others. And she canned apricots, sometimes with a stick of cinnamon or a few cloves; and she canned applesauce, quarts and quarts of it, and this was often from our own trees. All this fruit was canned in quart Mason jars, processed in a big pot on the wood-burning kitchen stove; and I would think nothing of sneaking into the tankhouse and prying up a lid with my fingernails and wolfing down an entire quart at a time, never thinking of the amount of work my poor mother had done.

In the summer we'd spend a Sunday all together picking blackberries in the willow copse down our road, big juicy black-berries that Mom always said were not really wild blackberries but Himalaya berries. We picked them by the gallon: I know, because I picked them into the three-gallon stainless-steel milk bucket, careful not to let it fall not so much lest it spill the ber-ries on the ground — you could always pick them back up again — but lest I dent this glorious shiny pail. I crawled far out onto the nearly horizontal limbs of the willows to pick ber-ries that had grown far up into the trees, avoiding the poi-sonoak that Dad was somehow luckily immune to, and that made Mom break out into a rash if she even got downwind of it.

And in the fall we picked up windfalls in the apple orchard across Blank Road, behind our mailbox, and tossed them into the farmer's apple-grinder, and then pressed out the cider. I suppose we were harvesting for him, and he was paying us in cider. In any case although the rotten apples were disgusting and the yellowjackets were threatening the cider was delicious, and Dad would set some aside in jugs to which he added brown sugar and raisins to make applejack which he enjoyed but I did not.

The months passed in this fashion, from the fall of 1945, when we settled on Blank Road, up until about the end of 1947. In September of that year another brother was born, Timothy, and Mom had her hands quite full, particularly when Jim fell sick and was diagnosed, by the patient Dr. Sharrocks, with tuberculosis. The rest of the family was quickly tested, and all showed up negative except me: there was a slight suspicion that I might be vulnerable, and I was shipped off to Gramp's again to spend a year and a half back in Berkeley.

circa 1947

3: Berkeley, 1948-1949

THIS WRENCH WAS THE MOST disturbing yet. I was set down in a completely different kind of family routine; postwar city life had evolved much further beyond the rustic life I'd been living; and, at twelve years, I was old enough to care about the obvious mismatches between me and the people around me, at home and at school.

Gramp and Gram had bought a twostorey stucco house on a quiet hillside street. A huge redwood tree shaded the front yard, but the back of the house, where the dining room was downstairs and my grandparents' bedroom was upstairs, looked out onto the bay and San Francisco and Mt. Tamalpais beyond, the Golden Gate Bridge closing the view at the center. The house was an interesting one: a bedroom and bathroom were set over the garage; upstairs there were three more bedrooms and a bath; downstairs a goodsized living room, dining room, and kitchen.

Best of all there was a staircase off the kitchen leading down into the basement, with a workbench and shelves for Gramp's collection of partially full cans of paint; and out the basement door a good-sized back yard on two terraces, with the clothesline, and a small lawn, and snowball bushes and camellias, plants that no doubt reminded Gram of the years in China, when they'd had a gardener and an amah and servants to help with the housework — though I never heard Gram talk about such things.

The first few months must have been devoted simply to adjusting. First there was the house and neighborhood to explore. On rainy days there was the basement to play in — "play" involving for the most part simply investigating everything, taking note of the tools and scraps of wood and leather and the brushes and cans of paint, seeing how they were arranged, taking in their shapes and colors. I see now that this is what I did; I'm sure I didn't investigate them thus with any consciousness. There had been plenty of tools at home; Dad was forever fixing and making things. But among the things he fixed were the tools themselves, for they had a way of scattering. We even evolved a goodnatured mantra concerning this: "First you find the tool. Then you find the tool you need to fix the tool. Then you fix the tool. Then you lose the tool."

Gramp wasn't like that: whether from the example of his own father or from long years in the chemistry labs at school, he kept a degree of casual order in his shop. There was even more order in the house itself, and I was expected to contribute to it. The hall closet had a set of shelves on which stood what seemed to be the entire run of the National Geographic, and these were in chronological order. (The earliest, in black and white, interested me the most, perhaps because they had the most photographs of unclad native women.)

The furniture in the living room was comfortable and comfortably placed, and one didn't play don't-touch-the-floor with it. There were a few *objets d'art* which I hadn't remembered from Bancroft Way, though I'm sure they were there: a framed sepia-tone photograph of a quiet stream with a few houses on its bank, which I later learned showed a place they'd lived in in China; a landscape painted on silk; a number of fat porcelain "household gods," I was told, with real hair streaming out their ears and nostrils. The piano was there, too, not yet quite interesting me — it had been years since my last lesson.

There were neighbors on our side of the street, but no other children. Mrs. Ricketts, on the south side, lived in a curious low flat-roofed house set with many windows; she made a terrible apple pie that she tried to entice me with, but she was simply too odd, and her house reeked with dander from her threatening though aging Airedale. There were a few kids around the corner, on Eunice Street, which ran precipitously downhill toward Spruce Street, and now and then I played games with them, Mother May I and Dodgeball and the like, but no real friendships developed there.

At school, though, I did have a couple of good friends. One was the good-natured Larry Rinne, whose father was a fireman, and who lived in a big house down on Francisco Street. He taught me to make a primitive mortar: you make a small hole in the center of the end of a soup-can, tape a firecracker inside the can, its fuse carefully threaded through the hole; and invert the can inside a larger one partially filled with water. When the firecracker goes off the soup-can sails impossibly high into the sky: we used to try, unsuccessfully, to break the streetlights with them. And it was in Larry's back yard that one day I heard my first jet airplane fly overhead, and was amazed that the airplane was so far ahead of its sound.

There was Robert Ek, who lived in a war-housing apartment by the railroad tracks down on Virginia Street, and who collected things, especially German war items: swastikas and eagles and spiked helmets and the like; and there was Bruce Flood, who played the bagpipes.

Best of all there was Wiley Keys, who I must have known earlier. His own house was amazing, for his father was an explorer, it seemed to me. His forbidden study, which we explored on tiptoe, was set about with elephant's-foot wastebaskets and Masai shields and spears, and there were enigmatic books in his locked glass-fronted bookcases. Under the rug, at the head of the dining table, there was a push-button which lit a signal in the kitchen so the maid would bring in the next course at dinner. His house was set far back from the street and surrounded by beautiful oak trees, and nearby there was Indian Rock Park, where we climbed and explored or simply lay on our backs on warm sunny days and admired the sky overhead.

Across the street from our own house was the creek and its waterfalls. Explorations here were difficult because of the poisonoak, but we took our chances. The creek led to the magnificent Berkeley Rose Garden, an amphitheater of terraces planted in rosebushes and capped by a curving redwood trellis covered with Joseph's Coats. At the bottom of the terraces there was a small pool fed by Codornices Creek: I used to "swim" in it, stripping to my underwear and half-floating, half walking on my hands. In those days the entire structure was still fairly new, barely ten years old, but it looked back to an entirely different age, unshadowed by the War.

And beyond the Rose Garden, after you passed the tennis courts not yet fully taken advantage of except on weekends, you went through a pedestrian tunnel to yet another park, Codornices Park, with a big flat playground that included a softball field at one end and a great sloping lawn at the other, on which we used to lie sideways and roll, faster and faster, down the hill, hoping no dogs had been there first.

Beyond the playground came the wilds, hillsides covered with blackberry bushes and bamboo thickets, split by Codornices Creek, and rising ultimately to the native chaparral and clearings of the Berkeley Hills east of the University Campus. Here we played Prisoner's Base and Capture the Flag, when there were enough of us, or we slid down the steep hillsides on flattened cardboard boxes, or simply explored.

All this was not so very different from play back on Blank Road, except for Wiley and Larry and Bob and one or two other friends. But school was bewilderingly different. I'd left Eucalyptus School halfway through the first semester of the eighth grade, bored and unchallenged: but at Garfield Junior High there was an entirely different approach to education, four or five hundred children were plunged into separate rooms devoted entirely to one class or another, and after forty-five minutes or so you went to another room, stopping off at your locker to change textbooks.

As if that weren't enough, there were other buildings. There was a big fairly new gymnasium, and behind and below it, down a steep hillside, a football field and track. There was no question of avoiding gym class here; no one played Andy Over or sat under a tree reading. We did calisthenics or played at basketball on rainy days, in the unpleasantly echoing noise of this huge gym; or we were forced into various team sports, scrimmaging on the football field or playing kickball on the asphalt playground between the main building and the gym.

There were also a few "temporary buildings," low gable-roofed wooden sheds divided into two rooms for the most part. I took something in one of these, perhaps a kind of singing class; and I remember seeing a boy running from another classroom, sobbing and holding a bloody handkerchief in his hands, the shop teacher running alongside carrying the poor boy's fingertip, for he'd cut it off in his wood shop class.

In three semesters at Garfield I took English and Algebra and, most useful of all, Typing, and I'm sure there was some kind of science class, Gramp wouldn't have let that go by; and even a class in some kind of theater; I think I had something to do with the sound part of it — there were times when I was setting up some sort of sound apparatus, and movie projectors. I took a semester of Art, too; we drew, mostly in pencil though occasionally in charcoal, using plaster casts of various sorts for our models. But of all this instruction I recall only vignettes: Mr. Van Meter going to the blackboard to expound on an algebraic formula, and, one day, yanking down on the belt of a boy who wore his jeans too low on his hips, probably accidentally pulling them down quite off his hips and exposing his underwear and shirt-tails, and then ordering the boy out of the classroom until he could learn to dress properly. For in those days decorum and discipline was expected in class; one didn't even whisper without earning a bad mark, and conversation in class was inconceivable.

I can see my drama teacher, a pretty young brunette named Mrs. Curtice, married, it was enviously said among us boys, to the principal of Berkeley High School. I can see my art teacher, who had a very plain, white face, and perfectly tweezed eyebrows perpetually astonished at our clumsiness, and a tight bun at the back of her head; it was rumored to be a wig. I can see old Mrs. Almy, who taught math in the upper eighth grade, and had trouble getting me to pay attention; and Mrs. Rowell, I think her name was, who taught English in the ninth grade, where we had to read *A Tale of Two Cities*, which depressed me so much I haven't read Dickens since.

For some reason I was made a hall monitor, which didn't do a lot for my popularity among the other kids. In some of the intervals between classes I was assigned to stand at one strategic location or another, in the middle of the hall, and make certain kids kept to the right as they rushed between classrooms. This may have been a sort of audition for an even more enviable position: Junior Traffic Patrol, which entitled you to a bright yellow-orange sweater, a service cap of similar color, and a stop-sign on a pole: at a signal you carried this out into the crosswalk, snapped to attention, and leaned your sign smartly away from your solidly planted foot, stopping all vehicular traffic until the schoolchildren had safely crossed the street, whereupon another blast on the whistle from the Traffic Patrol Sergeant, the most enviable position of all, would set you stiffly pivoting and marching back to the sidewalk.

The walk to school and home was very different in Berkeley, but still one of the best parts of the day. It was perfectly engineered: in the morning it was all downhill; you could skip or trot the distance in good time, and waste other minutes investigating side-trips, or socializing with a few friends — Larry and I used to flatten pennies on the F-train tracks, when we saw a train coming, and Larry had the ingenious idea of scratching fake Arabic markings into the resulting blank coins, and selling them at a quarter apiece to Bob Ek, who collected things, but was less discerning than he knew. On the way home we'd stop by the doughnut shop on Grove Street, partly for the doughnuts, which cost a nickel apiece, but mostly, as far as I was concerned, to marvel at the machine that nudged them slowly in a circular path in a pool of simmering oil, lifting them out and turning them over at the halfway point.

Machines had fascinated me back on Blank Road, even when they terrified me; I loved gears and wheels and belts and levers. (The fascination even dominated my sleep: for years I was troubled by a recurring nightmare, which found me sitting on a low curbstone, contemplating a coin in the gutter. I knew that if I touched it some terrible thing would ensue, but I couldn't help slowly bending down, taking it between thumb and forefinger, and slowly turning it other side up, whereupon the entire universe seemed to turn slowly into the inside of an enormous cement mixer, slowly grinding and turning and churning me and everything else with it.)

The city offered more surprising machines than those in Hessel: Gram's mangle, which she used every Tuesday to iron everything she'd washed the previous day, even my socks and underwear. Aunt Dorothy's Philco, the doughnut cooker, the streetcars. I became fascinated by model railroads, perhaps re-calling Guymon in my subconscious, or Dad, who used to sing about trains, no doubt recalling his own freight-train travel.

> *I used to go*
> *Down to the station*
> *Every evening just to watch that Pullman train come rollin' in*

We ate dry cereal at breakfast at Gramp's. This was some-thing entirely new; we'd never had anything but oatmeal or cornmeal mush at home. And one of these dry cereals enticed customers by printing cut-and-paste-together models on the back of the box, airplanes during the war, I suppose, but loco-motives and freight cars now, in 1948. I had a little money from an allowance, and I spent all of it on box after box of this cereal.

Gramp, when he discovered the models I'd put together, also discovered the waxed-paper liners of cereal I'd hidden some-where, not daring simply to throw it out; one didn't throw food away, and there were no chickens to give it to. He made me eat it all, or at least so much of it I never wanted any again, and that was the end of the model trains, at least for the moment.

But it wasn't the end of my fascination. One school friend lived on Shattuck Avenue in a big house later torn down for the erection of yet another supermarket; behind, in his back yard, his father had a model train — unheard of, that a grown-up would play with such things — on so big a scale that its tracks ran through the garden itself. And quite far away in my terms, all the way down Grove Street at University Avenue, there was a hobby shop, and here I'd spend an occasional dollar on a genuine scale-model kit. Gramp gave in, I think, when he saw that an occasional indulgence in this would lead me to learning useful shop routines. There weren't many opportunities, but I managed to put four or five freight cars together — box cars, re-frigerator cars: flat cars seemed a waste of money — and paint them in accurate representations of the originals, colors with exotic names like Venice Red and Raw Umber. I even managed to buy a foot or two of track, but a locomotive remained perma-nently out of reach, and I read the forbidden copies of Model Railroader magazine, thirty-five cents a copy, with a great deal of wistfulness.

Some of the money, though not much, came from my job. I had a real job! I delivered newspapers in the afternoon, the Oakland *Tribune*, my route taking me over to Virginia and even Cedar Street, up to Euclid, then uphill all the way to Eunice and a little beyond, cutting across back yards to Corona Court and Oak Street, then back along Arch toward home. This was pleasant enough on weekdays, if it wasn't raining: I enjoyed folding the papers into their flattened triangular packages, then tossing them up onto the porches. On Sunday, though, this was a real chore: you had to get up early, and spend an hour or so with boys you didn't like, inserting advertising supplements into the thick newspaper, and they were heavy and too cumbersome to fold, so you rolled them up as best you could and snapped a rubber band around them, and you had to carry them to many porches too distant to throw these weighty objects. And, halfway through your route, you had to stop at a streetcorner box and repeat the entire process, for there was no way you could carry sixty-five or seventy of these papers at a time.

Worst of all was collecting, at the end of the month, when a surprising number of subscribers would vanish. They'd been all too apparent otherwise, complaining about missed papers, or papers tossed into puddles or onto porch roofs: but when it was time to get a dollar or two from them they were nowhere to be seen, and you had to make repeated trips to the doorbell, embarrassed to be asking for money. So I didn't stay at the job long; Gramp probably got tired of hassling me Sunday mornings, when he had his own job to prepare for, for he was still an elder at church, and had to appear without paint under his fingernails or wiry grey whiskers poking through his wrinkled cheeks, which seemed to be his usual Saturday-night appearance.

Gramp was in many ways a second father to me. He taught me how to use the tools that Dad had simply expected me spontaneously to have mastered: Let the saw do the work, boy! Don't push so hard at it! For I'd been led to think you had to push the teeth into the wood, whereas a properly sharpened and set carpenter's saw actually *wanted* to bite into the wood; all you had to do was stand at exactly the right position, shoulder above saw-handle, and keep the blade perfectly straight.

Set your knee under the shovel-handle, boy! Use your head; this is a lever; take advantage of it! And shoveling dirt became a lesson in the three simple machines, lever, inclined plane, and pulley, of which the lever was the most magical because the simplest, and I began to see the structural relationship of levering a car out of the mud with a eucalyptus pole, on the one hand, and using a shovel to toss sand into the cement mixer, on the other.

Breakfast was that invariable dry cereal, usually with a sliced banana on it, and lunch was taken at school, in the cafeteria where I came to be known as Beet-Lover because I refused ever to eat them, leaving them bleeding at the edge of the plate. Dinners were plain, such things as macaroni and cheese and meat loaf; and afterward Gramp would put on an inappropriate ruffled apron and stand at the sink washing the dishes. Then he sat in his armchair, smoking a cigar — his one vice, that single cigar a day — and reading the newspaper, while Gram mended, darning socks — this was familiar; Mom had spent many evenings doing the same — and I read or did schoolwork or idled through a National Geographic.

We were one of the first families on our street to have a television set, and I was the only one who seemed capable of balancing its touchy controls: vertical hold, horizontal hold, contrast and brightness, and all that. The screen was small and, of course, monochrome, and there were few channels broadcasting, but we watched an hour or so most evenings. I remember watching the Ed Sullivan show: one night the soprano Marian Anderson was featured: She certainly is mighty ugly, Gramp said, But my heavens she can sing.

There was a fifteen-minute program every evening, I think, that featured a small orchestra playing the kind of music that was increasingly appealing to me. As their theme they played the scherzo of the Bizet Symphony in C, which had only recently been discovered; it remains a favorite piece, and perhaps formed my fondness for French rather than German music.

And we watched children's programs, particularly Kukla, Fran, and Ollie and Crusader Rabbit, countenanced by my stern grandparents because there were now two smaller cousins living with us. One night, after I'd gone to bed, I heard the telephone ring, and then Gram screaming. "Bob's dead! Bob's dead! Oh, Lord, Bob's dead!" This wasn't Uncle Bobby, whom I hadn't seen in years, but Aunt Barbara's husband, who'd died after surgery for a cerebral hemorrhage, whatever that was. And in a few days here was Aunt Barbara, who moved into Aunt Dorothy's now vacant mezzanine bedroom, and had brought her daughter Anne and her little boy Craig with her. I was no longer the only child in the house, and this was mostly a relief, because Gramp and Gram had other things to do than concentrate on my improvement, great though the opportunities were.

Anne and Craig had the big guest bedroom on the top floor, next to Gram and Gramp's; my bedroom was much smaller, under the eaves at the front of the house, shaded by the redwood tree. I was bigger now, and had more liberty — I turned a teen-ager in the late summer of 1948, after finishing the eighth grade. That summer I was sent to the YMCA camp near the mouth of the Gualala River, in Sonoma county. Gramp took me, I guess, to a gathering-place in San Francisco, I with my sleeping bag and a dufflebag of clothes, and with a number of other campers I was herded onto the bed of a flat-bed truck with stake sides, exactly as if we were cattle. It was a beautiful day. The truck stopped for some reason near the crest of the hill leading north from the Golden Gate Bridge, giving us a fine view of the bridge and the city, and then inexorably took us on, on, on.

We slept at camp in tent-cabins, spent the days learning to swim, to weave baskets of raffia, to do various woodcrafty things, to canoe. We took our meals in the big common dining hall, where I felt very grown-up because at breakfast we were served Postum, a synthetic coffee-like beverage I'd never had before. We sang around the campfire at night, and heard ghost stories. But one day I was running down a path through the forest and somehow riled a nest of hornets, and one flew into my left ear. I ran to the first-aid station and was immediately put in the back seat of someone's car, and we drove terrifyingly fast over the unpaved, narrow, winding Skaggs Spring Road to

Healdsburg, where drops of something were put in my ear and a doctor retrieved the hornet, finally dead, with a pair of forceps, while a very kind black man soothed me with conversation — he impressed me tremendously, as I'd never really spoken to a black man before; there were none in those days, in my life, outside of the shipyards.

Being bigger and stronger I was expected to work more, of course, and had to help Gramp paint and even do some building on Saturdays. Our most complex job was the building of an addition on the back of an apartment building up on Le Roy Avenue, an amazing street, I thought, with an oak tree growing in the middle of the street, and an exotic-looking glass-front studio building through whose windows I could see a grand piano, and a creek rushing down alongside; and when we sat on the curb, eating our sandwiches, we could hear the Campanile chimes, first telling the hour, then breaking into a great jumble of melody, the individual notes hanging on for different lengths of time and blurring into the air.

Gramp was clearing the vacant lot across the street from his own house, too, and Uncle Bobby showed up to help, for the first project was to build a small house for him to live in. Bobby and Gramp and Gramp's brother Percy cut away the brush, and I didn't have to help with this, because of the poisonoak; but when they stacked it in a great heap and burned it I somehow got into the smoke, and I missed nearly a month of school at the beginning of the ninth grade, swollen and bandaged and left in bed, for the smoke had got into my lungs and I had rashes and reactions inside and out.

But while I had more work to do, and while school was finally becoming more of a challenge, I also had more liberty. I even got into trouble, though I don't think any of the grownups ever knew, running around at night with a couple of other boys, stealing hub caps, sneaking through stranger's yards, exploring buildings under construction. I skipped out of church, too, staying long enough to be seen and to participate in the hymns, but evading the long sermon that followed. Instead I'd sneak out a side door and join Wiley for explorations of the University campus, which he knew well through his father's position on faculty, and which I remembered for those trips to the psychology building where I'd been tested so often.

I suppose a sort of dialectic began to grow in my subconscious between religion and knowledge. I still didn't read in any consistent way; *A Tale of Two Cities* was the first extended narrative I'd ever had to read; otherwise I'd read Lewis Carroll, of course, and *The Wind in the Willows*, and *The Water-Babies*; and a book that's remained a favorite, Charles Carryl's *Davy and the Goblin*. I'd read books about Greek mythology or astronomy or chemistry or the lives of scientists, all written especially for young readers. I knew Shakespeare's plots, for example, the few I did know, from the bowdlerized retellings by Charles and Mary Lamb. I'd read here and there in Edgar Allen Poe, in Mom's ancient set, still on my bookshelf, but it was the shorter tales that interested me, not the poetry (which had greatly interested her in her youth, I suddenly realize as I write this). I'd often stared at the Gustav Doré engravings in a copy of *The Divine Comedy*, though it never occurred to me to try to read it; the long pages of unbroken verse probably put me off; they still do.

There were a few pictures on the walls: a photograph of a narrow canal — perhaps no more than a drainage ditch — that ran behind some buildings, rather fuzzily photographed; I was told this represented a place in China, and it occurs to me now that it was perhaps an enlargement of a photo one of my uncles, the artistic Clay perhaps, had taken of a place they'd lived in. There was a needlepoint landscape, also from China. And hanging over the breakfast table a reproduction of Nicolas Maes' famous painting *Prayer*, showing an old woman thanking the Lord for her meager meal — I now know she represents an old woman, but her face so resembled Gramp's I took her to be a man for years afterward; early on I wondered if it weren't perhaps a picture of Gramp himself, or perhaps of *his* grandfather.

Gram and Gramp were religious, and their religious beliefs were a constant though not overweening part of our daily domestic life. Dinner always began with a short formulaic prayer — *Lord, bless this food we are about to eat* — and Gram read the Bible silently, in her rockingchair, fairly often. Church was oddly repugnant to me, not for anything it preached exactly, but something that rang false. Soon after moving in with Gram and Gramp, at Easter, 1948, being twelve years old, I was baptized; and I remember having misgivings at the idea of dedicating my life to something I didn't really understand. There was a curious sort of cabinet at the center of the back of the altar at University Christian Church, and I finally learned what it was: door-panels slid back to either side, revealing something seen only backstage, so to speak: a small pool, with steps leading down into it. On the day in question this was filled with unforgivingly cold water, and a number of us, wearing blue jeans, white shirts, and neckties, were led down the steps to be addressed by the preacher, who then placed one hand on my scalp, the other at the small of my back, and I lay back into the cold water and immediately stood back up, gracefully I hoped as far as the congregation could see, and I was now pure and redeemed, at least until the next time I did something unforgivably wrong.

We went nearly every Wednesday night to the Church Supper, sitting at long tables in the basement social hall scented faintly with wet concrete and long-cooked carrots. Here it was only the kitchen that pleased, with its huge stoves and ovens, the long work-table set with Pyrex dishes and Revere-ware pots of chicken a la king, peas with pearl onions, tuna casserole, and innumerable versions of gelatin salads, for these Wednesday-night dinners were potlucks, and the ovens were used only for the final baking of round tins of dinner rolls and the occasional pineapple upside-down cake.

I think I remember Gram taking me to be fitted with my Sunday-go-to-meeting suit, shortly after arriving fresh from the country. We took the streetcar downtown to The House of Harris, with its friendly sign Call Me Joe, a cut-price haberdashery at the south, downtown end of that curious block of businesses that stood like an island, recalling the train station that had been there decades earlier, where Shattuck Avenue runs into University Avenue.

Other shopping expeditions introduced me now and then to the outside world. We went occasionally to Hink's department store, whose pneumatic tubes to the cash desk upstairs were a source of wonder and delight. In the basement we would visit with a friend of Gram's, a slim woman with severely dressed dark hair and a serious but friendly expression, always dressed in knits for she ran the knitting department, with its arrays of vividly dyed skeins of yarn: I used to sit for hours at a time, it seemed, skeins of yarn suspended between my outstretched hands, watching Gram or Aunt Barbara wind the yarn into balls. Why did they do that, I wondered, not realizing the snarls that would otherwise result when the knitting began.

Across the street stood the Egyptian-style public library, where I'd been taken years earlier when I was in kindergarten, I suppose, or even earlier, to sit on the floor in front of the fireplace in the children's wing upstairs, listening to stories read aloud. Now I was much older, in Junior High School, and went there only to accompany Anne and Craig.

And occasionally we would go even further, Gram and I, taking the streetcar all the way down Shattuck Avenue and then Telegraph Avenue, past the mysteries of the Home for the Blind where she occasionally bought a broom, all the way down to Oakland, where she bought herbs from a Chinese pharmacist to treat her increasingly crippling rheumatism; or we visited the creaky wooden escalators of Capwell's Department Store, or one memorable time investigated the Crystal

Palace Market, a huge, noisy, smelly, confusing jumble of stalls selling fruits and vegetables, fish and meat, in a Babel of languages and races within a dirty glass-and-iron building soon then to be demolished to make way for a parking lot.

This was the time when streetcars were giving way to the automobile, the big noisy dirty buses being society's unwilling sop to those too poor to buy a car. Gram never learned to drive, and Gramp rarely participated in these shopping expeditions, needing his Saturdays to earn a few extra dollars. Aunt Barbara had a car, the first of many Oldsmobiles she would buy over the years; and now and then took me on expeditions of her own. In warm weather she took me, with Anne and Craig, to a swimming hole she favored in remote Contra Costa County, undoubtedly a place she'd known when she was in college before she married Bob, a dammed creek on the eastern slopes of Mt. Diablo; and at least once she took me out to Bob's family's farm in the Central Valley somewhere out near Modesto, where we ate watermelon fresh from the fields. I was even taken out there once by Gramp and Gram: the ride took us out Macarthur Boulevard, then edged with neat, well-maintained cottages and bungalows, and then down country roads shaded by huge oaks, and through walnut groves and apricot orchards; the country seemed more fertile, more gardened than the country we lived in in Sonoma County, whose beauty was wilder and more recalcitrant.

My body was changing, in ways too subtle for others to notice, I hoped, but distressfully for me. Aunt Barbara used to bathe Anne and Craig together, and once came into the mezzanine bathroom when I was in the tub; I quickly covered myself with the washcloth. What do you have to be ashamed of, she asked, undoubtedly meaning something humorous to apologize for her own accidental intrusion, but the question stayed with me for years. It is a literal question, posed by the world at large, and it is full of many meanings: What is it that you have; is there an obligation to be ashamed; what is it in you that contravenes some kind of expectation.

The entire matter of sexuality was both enigmatic and vaguely repellant. Of course I'd witnessed plenty of examples of animal breeding, but it seemed unlikely the physical act of generation could have much to do with the ongoing relationships and preoccupations of the people I lived among. One day Gram brought me a book from the small library at church; it was meant to educate people my age in sexual matters, but I couldn't get past the rather silly frontispiece of a male dog, sitting on his hindquarters, displaying his equipment with the usual foolish doggy smile on his face. What could this have to do with me?

There was no sex play among my friends, that I knew of, and I didn't form any friendships with girls. My only contact with girls my own age were Anastasia, who had moved away with her parents to Palo Alto. Joanne and Claudia didn't often visit, though from time to time I saw Joanne, blonde and popular and beautiful, sipping an ice-cream soda with a number of friends at McCurdy's, down on Shattuck and Vine. Claudia was something of an invalid, often in bed with an asthma attack; and my cousins Roxanne and Anne were even younger than she.

Anastasia had been taken by her parents to Palo Alto, where Bob Martin had opened his own record shop. Nor did I see, during this stay in Berkeley, anything of Edith and Will, who had relocated to Alhambra, an inconceivable distance away. They seem to have grown distant from Mom and Dad, if only because of the long trip required to visit — in those days the highway consisted of two lanes, and the wait for the ferry could be long. Blank Road was increasingly isolated from Berkeley, though I did make occasional trips back, for weekends and holidays I suppose. Once I rode up with Uncle Clay, who paid the ferry toll with a hundred-dollar bill, and who stopped midtrip at a strange restaurant in Novato, and who asked me, while he was driving, to hand him a bottle of water that lay on the floor under my seat.

There was one long trip, too, all the way down to Alhambra, during a Christmas vacation I think; Edith's brother Curt drove, and I sat in the back seat with a nephew or cousin of his, another boy about my age, and marveled at the scenery — we drove down highway 101, past lettuce fields and fruit orchards, past the huge Army base, through rolling hills, and spent a night in a motel in San Luis Obispo, whose setting fascinated me, tucked into a long valley running the wrong way. I suppose we visited the Mission, but I don't recall it; it was the natural landscape that held my attention.

But he embarrassed me on the drive down to Los Angeles, asking me and the other boy about things that I didn't think it right to talk about. And on another occasion he took me on a long hike, for he was practicing in some way, I was told, for the summer, when he'd be taking a troop of Boy Scouts on a camping expedition. We took a bus up to a town n the Santa Cruz Mountains, and walked from there to Santa Cruz, hiking along disused railroad tracks, and spending the night, I think, in sleeping bags. When I did something wrong — walked too slow, or stumbled — he made me strip naked and do push-ups. There was something uncomfortable about it.

But during that period, when I was in eighth and ninth grade, I spent most of my time in Berkeley. Uncle Lester had bought a house across the street, at 1245 Glen, and I spent long days helping him build a rather elaborate patio behind it. First we poured a concrete pavement, and it was my job to shovel in the sand, gravel, and cement, being careful to get the proportions correct, for he had a witheringly sarcastic way of expressing displeasure. Then he bought a load of old cobblestones somewhere, and I carried them, one by one, from the street, up the steep driveway, and around the house on a narrow path, to the back yard, where he built retaining walls of them. For a time I slept in that house, on a sleeping porch with a large screened opening looking out over the creek; this was one of the most pleasant bedrooms I've slept in.

At about the same time Gramp and Bobby and Percy built a little house, magically set right over the creek, for Bobby to live in, I think. I don't recall helping with this; I must have been too young still. Then, next door to Dorothy and Lester's house — by now I was getting old enough to drop the honorific "Aunt" and "Uncle" when I spoke to my aunts and uncles — Gramp was building another house, with Lester's occasional help, and Percy's. When it was finished Dorothy and Lester moved in, rented out the old one, and began building yet another. Soon enough a row of three houses had replaced the streetside entrance to what had been jungle and wilderness before. The ancient wood one-car garage, with its oil-stained wood-plank floor, where I had cut firewood from California bay branches with a bow-saw and sawbuck, was gone, and by the time I was fourteen I was learning about nostalgia.

(l-r) Jim, Mom, CS, John, Dad, Tim, ca. 1950

4: High School, 1949-1952

THEN IT WAS JUNE 1949, and I graduated from Garfield Junior High School. I don't remember ever wondering where I would go to high school; such decisions had always been made for me. I don't remember whether I wanted to stay in Berkeley or to return to Sonoma county; and I don't remember really feeling that either one or the other was in any sense my own place, or that either my parents or my grandparents was my real family. There didn't seem to be any ongoing focus to life; life consisted of daydreams, or chores that would be repeated the next day. My grandfather and other adults might build a house, and when it was finished see that it was an accomplishment; but even something as considerable as that would almost immediately be followed by another similar project; there didn't seem to be any goal, any end to activity of any kind.

Jim had recovered from his tuberculosis; John was now four years old; Tim was nearly two; and Mom was unaccountably expecting her fifth child. This was news to me; I don't recall such things ever being talked about at home. I imagine my grandparents were troubled by this turn of events — Mom was fragile and life on Blank Road was hard — but they talked about it out of my hearing. Somehow, though, it was decided that I'd go back to the country for high school; perhaps to help out a little at home.

So having just turned fourteen myself I was plunged into another absolutely new social confusion, both at school and at home, where the little brothers were considerably more present than they'd been before, and more of a responsibility than younger cousins had ever been. Mom was pale and tired; Dad worked longer hours, getting home barely in time for the evening milking. The house was more comfortable: Dad had reconfigured its interior once again, to give Jim a sunnier room of his own for his long confinement to bed; and electricity had been brought in, apparently because the county government had agreed that a tuberculosis sickroom had to be provided for, even at community expense.

We continued to use wood for heating, though, and as I recall for cooking, and the house was still pretty rustic, with holes large enough for birds to fly in (and warm air to escape in winter), and at one time a litter of skunks under the living-room floor. With electricity television had come, and Dad watched boxing matches, whose noisy violence offended my growing sensitivities. The contrast between Gramp's home and Dad's spoke volumes, and I found myself preferring Berkeley. But a wonderful new thing had entered my life, and for the next three years dominated it. I fell in love with music.

I think I'd wanted to take up a musical instrument even when at Garfield, but for some reason had not been allowed to — perhaps my record of inattentiveness to violin and piano lessons was responsible, though I think Gramp was already worried that I'd turn out to have scholarly interests in a frivolous subject, not the math or physics he wanted me to follow. I picked out tunes on the piano on Glen Avenue, and even wrote a hymn once, inventing what seemed to me a new melody and trying to harmonize it as the church hymnal suggested all music was meant to be made. When I showed it to Gram, though, Gramp seemed unimpressed. Barbara too. Gram was gratifyingly appreciative, but then she was always supportive; her approval didn't really count. So I didn't repeat the experiment.

At Analy Union High School, though, "music" meant a band, and I learned to play wind instruments. They proved to be much more suited to me, or I to them, than the piano or the violin. Hand and finger placement, the natural dependency of the phrase on one's breathing; above all the restriction of the instrument to only one note at a time — suddenly the instrument was an accomplice, not a device to be mastered and subdued. On the first day of school I was apprehensive and excited when fifth period came and I found my way to the music room, a cavernous room, well lit by twostorey steel-frame windows on three sides, with mysterious closet-like rooms off the fourth side, practice rooms from which bleats and blats could be heard from saxophones, clarinets, and trumpets in the hands of rank beginners.

Mister Knight asked me what I wanted to learn to play, looking surreptitiously at my hands and jawline. Bassoon, I said, remembering Grandpapa in Prokofiev's *Peter and the Wolf*, one of the small number of record albums on our shelves at home. It didn't occur to me to wonder whether there'd be a bassoon, but of course there was, and Mr. Knight was very happy to entrust me with it. I wonder when it had last been played. He set the case carefully down on a table and opened its flat rectangular lid, hinging it all the way back flat against the table.

The bassoon was a marvelous object. It lay in sections, nestled in the deep blue plush of the case; long pieces and short ones, thin ones and wide, dark mahogany with lighter maple-color stripes, and an amazing clutter of shiny nickel-plated rods and keys and pads, and an intriguingly curved nickel-silver bocal; and, in a hidden pocket of the case, a couple of bassoon reeds in their plexiglas tubes, wads of cotton at the bottoms to protect the fragile reed, and little cans of fragrant wax and lubricant. This wasn't simply a musical instrument, it was a system and a structure, a thing to be assembled and maintained and cared for; not a machine to make sound with, but a companion whose collaboration might at times be truculent and resistant but would nevertheless provide me with hours of satisfyingly immediate pleasure while undertaking a long course of apprenticeship.

Until now the only times I'd really felt both myself and at ease, with no unwelcome distraction from other people, was when I was outdoors, in the fields or the forests around our house, or the parks in Berkeley. Here was an entirely new way of being lost in a rich system that was both intelligent and sensuous. Until now music had been a matter of phonograph records, the sounds enticing but mechanical; or else it had been a part of church, the singing text-driven and the organ accompaniment as mechanical as any phonograph. Now, though, it was an extension of breath and fingers. In fifth period it was entirely my own doing, as I learned the scales and arpeggios; and then soon enough in first period, when I took Band, it was an integration of my effort with the group.

I suppose I didn't get into the band that first week. That must not have happened until the spring semester, the beginning of 1950 — *Things will be nifty... in nineteen-fifty*, my father had sung the previous year, with the hopefulness that had led him, the year before that, to *things will be fine, in forty-nine*. That first semester at Analy High had been traumatic. The English teacher turned out to be the identical twin of the wire-spectacled old lady at Garfield, and unaccountably insisted on the freshman class, a year retarded compared to Berkeley, reading *A Tale of Two Cities*. Mom managed to get me excused from this, and I never took a class in English again until years later in my second year of college.

I couldn't get out of math and science, though; these were state requirements. Analy High only offered five periods of instruction, and two of these would be wasted, as I saw it, on these difficult and irrelevant studies. And there was History to memorize, and at some point, whether that first year or later, when I'd been allowed to drop math after nearly failing geometry, Spanish.

In addition to the studies of course I had to get used to a new group of fellow-students, virtually none of whom seemed remotely friendly or interesting. And in truth I must have been bewildering to them, oddly dressed and disheveled and utterly uninterested in football. Of course I was a year younger than anyone else, and I lived at virtually the end of the school district. Once the rains had set in I'd have been soaked and muddy when the bus arrived, a mile from my house, at the wooden platform we used to set the cans of cream on to be taken away; I remember squatting under the platform to try to keep dry until the bus came. Then it would lurch and hesitate seven circuitous miles to school, and I'd try to get the mud off my trouser-legs and stow my boots in my locker and hope somehow to blend into the crowd, until finally I gave that up as hopeless and took refuge instead in being different.

And then, soon after the semester had begun, I was summoned into the principal's office and told that the baby had come, that Mom was all right, but something was wrong with the baby, and I was to wait in the office until Dad came to take me to see Mom at the hospital.

It was a baby girl, the girl Mom and Dad had hoped for four years earlier; but she was too late. Each of my brothers had weighed a pound less than his predecessor at birth, and John I think was the last really healthy baby; Tim was born with a badly wandering eye, and Martha, named for Grandma, was born with an incompletely formed heart, I think: she was what was then called a "blue baby," starved for oxygen — a condition easily corrected now, but fatal then.

I never saw her, as she never came home from the hospital. She went from Palm Drive Hospital in Sebastopol, where I'd spent a few days recovering from my earlier burns, to Stanford Hospital, where there must have been some kind of special surgery team for such cases: but she did not survive, and was buried a few weeks later in the Sebastopol cemetery.

I wasn't there. Mom and Dad never spoke about her, at least not in my hearing. It was another of those things that caused Mom to bite her lip, silently; and Dad to come home later from work. Sickness, sorrow, and defeat were not matters for public discussion. I suppose this may have been a design to keep me from suffering, to give me an optimistic or perhaps merely practical mental outlook. Mom must have got this from her Scottish-descended father and her patiently suffering mother; Dad may have fallen in with it out of what had been a youthful rejection of the misery of an absent father, a hard-scrabble life, his baby sister's early death. In any case it didn't seem to be a matter for my concern; I hardly knew about any of it. I took refuge in the bassoon.

Thinking about health and sex education as I experienced it I'm amazed at my family's silence. Mom and Dad were silent on most issues; indeed entire days seemed to go by without conversation of any kind. I suppose as the years passed the differences in their interests and enthusiasms, as they'd been established in the crucial formative years, when they not only did not know one another but could hardly have imagined the worlds in which one another were growing up — the differences must have grown more substantial than any shared experience. The year in Oklahoma had confirmed, I think, Dad's separation from Mom's family. Mom's relationship to Dad's had hardly existed until then, and was severed again when we settled on Blank Road.

Dad's worlds centered on two areas, his work, which remained an almost complete mystery to me; and the endless wheel-spinning work on the place, trying to make the house habitable, the outbuildings sufficient, the animals productive. Since the end of war work at the shipyards, Mom's world was centered on homemaking, and this did not really mean child care, at least as far as I was concerned. It was undoubtedly different with Jim, whose illness had given her a substantial responsibility — teaching as well as caring for him. But by then I was gone, and when I returned the family seemed to have gone through something that had changed its dynamics entirely.

During the three years I was in high school my parents' relationship went from bad, I would say, to worse. There was less and less communication. At the dinner table Mom invariably opened the conversation: *How was your day at work*. It seemed more a formula than a question, and rarely elicited anything of interest from my father. The dinner would proceed in silence. At the end, as Dad finished the bread he'd torn up and put into his tumbler of buttermilk — a tumbler which earlier had contained cheap Port wine — Mom would conclude the conversation: *Did you get enough to eat*. And that would be that. Mom spent long hours late at night standing at the window, looking moodily out at the night, smoking. I think she was waiting until Dad fell asleep before going to bed. It was all quite disturbing if I thought about it, so I didn't.

The Blank Road experiment had begun with great enthusiasm and optimism in the fall of 1945, at the dawn of the postwar period; it was winding down, though I didn't realize that yet, only five and six and seven years later, a victim of sickness, death, drudgery, overwork, and failure. And then Dad was drinking more, almost always alone and more or less in secret at home, after a drink or two in a bar on his way home from work. Bottles were hidden in the cars, and in various places in the outbuildings. His temper was growing ungovernable and I was afraid of him, so I protracted my absence at school, inventing reasons to dally with friends afterward. When I misbehaved I was pummeled a bit, until the terrible night I could stand this no longer and threw him to the floor, pinning his hands to the floor, kneeling over him, and telling him I would no longer submit to his tyranny. We both wept: it was a cruel and memorable moment full of regret and remorse for both of us.

Mom seemed a person apart. She seemed to spend a lot of time outside, her tanned face shaded by the pith helmet she often wore, tending her strawberry bed or her beehives. While I was at school she must have been busy with baking, canning, mending. She had time to sew, using a foot-treadle Singer: I remember hating the shirt she made from a cotton printed in too bold and too brown a pattern for my taste. Electricity had made her life a bit easier: she no longer had to fight a gasoline-engine powered washing machine, for example; and I think by now we had a normal hot-water heater. But she had an arduous life, and must have regretted the now distant world she'd given up: friends, poetry, painting. She cherished a few old books, among them a survey of Italian painting, and an edition of Walter Scott; and I remember gazing mystified at her dressing-table, whose drawers had unfinished cameos and costume jewelry she never wore.

This contrasted with a life that was often harsh. I hated having to work with the pigs: holding down the young ones while Dad castrated them, then smeared pungent pine-tar on their wounds; chasing them across the neighbor's pastures when they got out; finally butchering them. One night Dad and I had to find one that got away, and when we came to the neighbor's huge dairy barn Dad yelled for me to go on one side with the flashlight while he ran along the other side. I heard a strange sloppy sound, and then Dad's long litany of swearing, and went around to his side to find he'd blundered into the ma- nure pile up to his armpits and was struggling to get out: I couldn't help bursting out laughing, and then, scared at his re- sponse, ran home to wait for him to show up, either still furious or, more likely, either resigned to the situation or perhaps even laughing at it himself.

Butchering was particularly unpleasant. Dad usually got pretty drunk first, and then there'd be attempts to kill the poor beast, either shooting at it with an entirely inadequate .22 rifle or hitting it on the head with a sledge-hammer. Then there'd be the throat-slitting, and then we'd have to wrestle it into a vat of water boiling away on top of a wood fire; and then the shav- ing, and the cutting up, and the rendering of the lard...

Once Dad cut the tendons of three fingers on his right hand, stabbing the knife into the side of the barn where he'd have it handy, and we had to finish the job before he'd consent to drive into town to be treated. And another time he told me to put the pig's head in the icebox on the back porch — this was before we'd got electricity — and tell Mom he wanted her to make headcheese.

Tell him I won't open that icebox as long as that head is in it, she said. And a month later Dad tied a rope to the icebox and towed it down to the gully where we buried dead calves and household garbage, and it was never spoken of again.

There were of course pleasant moments as well, even moments involving work with Dad, cutting firewood or working on the various cars. Somewhere he'd come into an ancient truck, a 1902 model with an enormous, loud, slow engine that burned not real gasoline but kerosene. It had hard-rubber tires, so it couldn't legally be driven on the paved road, but this didn't matter, it wasn't likely to get that far anyway. It served chiefly to power our table-saw. And there was a series of other cars. One lacked a fuel pump for a while, and it was my job to ride perched on the engine cowling in front of the windshield, holding a jug of gasoline with a rubber tube, directing a steady drip of gas into the carburetor. Once it took fire, and Dad scolded me for abandoning ship: he simply scooped up dirt from the side of the road and smothered the flames, then started up again to continue the trip.

He wrecked a number of these cars. Once he ran one into the ditch, having been distracted by a bee that had flown under his clothing. His driving was erratic. I remember him lighting a cigarette with the dashboard lighter, then blowing on it and throwing it out the window: he was capable of that kind of absent-mindedness, and I found it endearing, and truth to tell I don't think he minded my delight. As irascible and stubborn as he could be — not to mention drunk and disorderly — he was a charming man, a man who craved sympathy and attention, and immensely polite and even courtly when he didn't feel crossed. You could see what it was attracted Mom to him, fifteen or twenty years earlier, before everything began to go all to hell.

And he had real musical talent, though he didn't read a note of music. When I arrived home with my bassoon he looked on with curiosity and admiration as I assembled it, moistened the reed, and began to squawk unpleasant blasts on it. He never touched the bassoon himself, but there wasn't an instrument I brought home later that he couldn't pick up for the first time, blow experimentally on it, and then improvise or even play a recognizable tune. In the next three years I learned all the woodwinds except the flute; and the French horn and tuba as well; and he could play any of them better than I could until I'd had them a few days.

His favorite instruments, though, were the accordion, the harmonica, and the Jew's harp. I never heard the tune when he plunked away on the latter instrument; it seemed to be completely internal to the player. I did not like the harmonica, which was always out of tune and wheezy; but at least Dad could not sing while playing it. When he played accordion or guitar he often sang, maudlin old cowboy songs for the most part, and these seemed insufferably low-life to me, and I went outside, or tried to shut myself into my bedroom to read.

I was getting bigger and stronger, even before that terrible night that I bested my father, and I was given a bigger share of the work. I could use an axe almost as well as Dad could, and I put in my share of hours with the garden tractor and the scythe. I had learned to drive, first on a Model T Ford — an example of Dad's insistence on the most primitive and irrelevant technology available — and then on the big 1929 Whippet touring car we had for a while, whose steering wheel came off in my hands as we descended Fat Lady Hill, whereupon Dad quickly clamped a pair of Vice-grips on the end of the steering column and shouted at me to steer with it. I may not have learned much by way of refined auto-mechanic's skills, but I learned to improvise and to make do, and the spirit of *bricolage*, as I later learned to call it, became a central part of my own set of survival skills.

Reading had progressed far beyond my earlier enthusiasms — The Curly-Tops, then the Oz books, and everything Ernest Thompson Seton wrote about childhood and woodcraft and the wonders of Nature. Someone, probably Gramp or Will Irwin, had provided me with popular science books: George Gamow's *One, Two, Three, Infinity*; and *Flatland*; and a charming book called *The Education of T.C. Mits*; and these made me fascinated with the images and vocabulary of science and mathematics, if not with the discipline and focus their mastery required.

And, of course, music continued to fascinate me: music from school, popular songs on the radio, Dad's few old 78 rpm shellacs of Jimmy Lunceford and Paul Weston, the fox trots with vocal refrain and the big-band swing, and the book of Gilbert and Sullivan we had, with descriptions of complex and exotic plots, and piano arrangements of the principal songs, many of which I memorized, wondering often at their mysterious words.

> *When he had Rhenish wine to drink*
> *It made him very sad to think*
> *That some, at junket or at jink*
> *Must be content with toddy.*

I spent three years altogether at Analy High, and after that first semester every possible moment was spent at music. I barely tolerated the other classes, which were required; and I didn't do very well in them. I was, of course, on a pre-college track, so I took science and language, where many of the other kids, certainly not the ones I spent any time with, were taking shop and agriculture.

I had to take physical education, and spent every possible minute simply running around the track. My lack of enthusiasm for team sports was strictly a result of my unwillingness to expose myself to new acquaintances. I hated the locker room and even the showers, though they were by far the best plumbing available to me in those years. On rainy days we had to spend the gym period in the gymnasium, playing basketball or doing calisthenics, and I hated the smell of sweat and varnish, the glaring light bouncing off the polished floor, and especially the hard and echoing noise. In better weather I was content to do my twenty laps of the track, five miles in all, and finally, since everyone had to be on a team of some kind, I was allowed to be a distance runner, though I somehow managed never to go to an interscholastic meet. The best season for crosscountry running was when the cherries were ripe, toward the end of the semester: I got into trouble on that score once, but my sentence wasn't harsh: more laps.

I barely got through my geometry class, where the stern but good-humored Miss Weseen, she of the steelrim glasses and tightly curled grey hair, scolded my inattentiveness but was oddly impressed with my idiosyncratic proof of the Pythagorean Theorem, the longest she had ever seen, she said, but without an unnecessary step in its convoluted logic. I wanted to take French but was sent instead to take Spanish, which was thought to have more eventual practical value: this was the first of many languages I have tried to learn over the years, with equal lack of success, due to my impatience with any kind of learning that didn't come either immediately or intuitively or, preferably, both at once.

Chemistry interested me. I had always been attracted to its fragrant mysteries, probably since my first exposure to Gramp's chosen profession. I remember once his taking me with him to spend the day at Mission High in San Francisco, where he taught all those years: he set me to entertain myself with textbooks and even a spectroscope, and I was fascinated by the orderly scales of color on the spectrographs. (I learned much later that spectrography was his particular field when he was in college; the discovery of so many of those elements through spectral analysis was then a matter of living memory.)

But while the laboratory experiments were fun and intriguing the arithmetic involved in all those chemical equations was too numbing for me, and I did badly in chemistry, as I had the previous year in biology, and would the following, final year of high school in physics. By then I was however in a very small elite indeed; there were only seven other kids in the physics class in this rural high school, and at a reunion of my graduating class, fifty years later, I met only one other classmate who'd gone into a profession: all the others had taken up trades, or stayed with the farming and dairying they'd grown up among.

Even the music department suffered from the practical, blue-collar orientation of this small rural high school, whose seven hundred students came from isolated farms and villages and lumber-towns miles to the north, west, and south of Sebastopol. When we first settled on Blank Road, in 1945, the first thing Mom did with respect to my education was to get me moved from the quite isolated but somewhat nearer one-room Canfield School to the relatively more advanced two-room school in Hessel. But I suppose she was too exhausted by now, too distracted by an increasingly troubled marriage, by the demands of children and babies and pregnancy, too preoccupied with the hardships of daily life, to fight for my admission to a more sophisticated high school. Petaluma, to the south, was just as close as Sebastopol, and of course Santa Rosa would have been another possibility, Dad drove to Santa Rosa every weekday to go to work. But we were in the Analy Union High School District, and there it was I went.

The chief disadvantage of this, to me, was the failure of the school to provide stringed instruments. We had no orchestra; we were a Band school. There was in fact one cello, and for a time Mr. Knight offered to give me a little instruction on it. But it was clear his heart wasn't in it, and for all I know he didn't know much about it himself. Mr. Knight was a good, gentle, prematurely gray, friendly man; he gave me every moment he could spare, and followed the bassoon, once I'd mastered the easiest keys (all flat, of course, since there was no orchestra here), with other instruments. I quickly learned enough alto saxophone, then baritone, to be able to play it during the fall semester, when all the band energies went into trying to inspire the loyal but disappointed fans of our demoralized football team at, playing fight songs and flourishes in the stands and marching through intricate formations at half-time.

That activity took me to neighboring high schools every other week: to Petaluma, Santa Rosa, Healdsburg, and as far away as Cloverdale; and here of course I could and certainly did take mental note of the position of our own band among this greater musical society. On two occasions we went even further, to an assembly of high school football bands in Vallejo, where we played en masse, several hundred of us, and began dramatically by playing the National Anthem in the dark, a spotlight picking out the proud American Flag fluttering above the stands — I did not have the Anthem by heart, and merely stood with my bassoon, I hadn't yet taken up the saxophone, at rest position; and a newspaper photographer recorded the moment with a flash camera, and there I stood, the only boy not playing, on a page of the Vallejo newspaper, to my father's great amusement.

Another time we participated in the half-time activities at the East-West Game, a postseason game of some importance played in those days in Kezar Stadium in San Francisco, not far from where my brother Jim had been born a dozen years earlier; and for this we had been endlessly coached and rehearsed, and our participation in the massed exercises seemed faultless to me, and our own choreographed routines up with the best and most complex of the competition.

But I lived for the spring semester, when there was no football, and we concentrated on concert music. Mr. Knight was as enthusiastic about this as I was, but he knew the limitations of his resources and his audience. We didn't go in for long pieces or for band transcriptions of orchestral repertoire. Instead we prepared cunningly balanced programs with novelty numbers and popular items relieved by occasionally more serious or at least dramatic compositions. We played arrangements of popular pieces by, for example, Leroy Anderson: "The Typewriter Song," "Trumpeter's Lullaby.." We played an arrangement of a suite by Ferde Grofé, not the *Grand Canyon Suite* but another stitching together tributes to various regional American musics or cities, I forget which. We played a very dramatic overture, as I thought it, by Paul Creston, intriguingly called *Zanoni*; I always wondered what the title meant. We played a band transcription of Harl McDonald's "Rhumba" Symphony. We played a novelty mambo that required us to grunt at certain key downbeats.

We played, most memorably for me, "The Teddy-Bears' Picnic," and Johann Strauss's "Perpetuum Mobile," and, every graduation ceremony, not "Pomp and Circumstance" but, oddly, "Entrance and March of the Peers" from Gilbert and Sullivan's *Iolanthe*. Why were these the most memorable? Because they featured the bassoon in exposed or difficult passages, and I did my best to get those passages down. Only a few measures of the "March of the Peers" eluded me, because it went into the tenor clef, and I'd never given it the attention I should have — for I'd already quite firmly given up routine practicing of scales and passages, preferring to sight-read new material. A superficial acquaintance with something previously unknown was always preferable to constant reminder of inadequate mastery of the familiar.

Our concert band met first thing in the morning, in that big band room smelling vaguely of sweat and the Celotex used for acoustical treatment. Instruments were stored in their cases on shelves in an adjacent room, quickly crowded by jostling students fresh from the school buses, all, as I remember, eager and enthusiastic. Kenneth E. Knight was well liked. We all called him "Kck," for his monogram, signed on so many permission slips for students needing special dispensation to leave another class early, or skip an otherwise mandatory assembly.

He was rather short, a little stocky, grey, with slightly rounded shoulders and a habit of peering up over his reading-glasses. We began each morning with a careful tuning, by section, Merton Tyrrel's oboe sounding a B flat (for this was a band, remember, and we did not play in the sharp keys that an "A" would imply); and then Kek would lead us through a few Bach chorales, to get both the pitch and the balance of the various sections into our ears.

We had a pretty good concert band, the best, I would have said, in our county; and every spring we had an opportunity to hear all our competition. It was on such an occasion that I heard my first live orchestra, if we don't count the one that played the Kitty-Cat Waltz on Treasure Island. That was the student orchestra at Santa Rosa High School, who attempted the "Waltz of the Flowers" from *Nutcracker*. There was a pretty good harpist at Santa Rosa High, the daughter of the local private music-teacher, who also conducted the Santa Rosa Symphony for many years. But they did not have much of a French horn section, and after the introductory harp roulades there was eight bars of oom-pah-pah accompaniment, the horn quartet anxiously silent after an initial flurry of false notes, before the clarinetist entered with his florid response to the absent melodic line.

We had at least one decent French horn player, and he was my other close friend throughout high school. Dick Brodt and Merton Tyrrel couldn't have offered more contrast, with the rest of the students or with each other — or, for that matter, with me. Merton was intellectual, rather formal, quite elegant, his dark hair slicked back from a high forehead, a lively eye but a rather cautious expression on his face. He played oboe, and excelled at math and science. He drew the single "A" in our physics class, when the rest of us all got "C"s, except for one poor fellow who failed in order to establish a perfect bell-shaped curve when the final grades were posted.

I only visited Merton's home once, when I think I was

dropped off to be taken to some event together with him. It was a small but very neatly maintained cottage on a gravel driveway, neatly clipped shrubbery in place, a smiling mother in an apron. And Merton, as I recall, never visited my home; I was probably too embarrassed to suggest such a visit.

Dick, on the other hand, lived in a squalor that surpassed even ours. His father, or perhaps adoptive father, I was never clear about that, was short and fat, unshaven, wore perpetual mattress-ticking bib overalls, and smoked a foul corncob pipe. His mother was big and blowsy, and there was a bevy of half-brothers and -sisters who had little to do with Dick and less to do with me. They lived in what had until recently been a chickenhouse on Bloomfield Road, which was on my school bus route; so we shared part of that ride in addition to mutual visits at home. Dick and I played endless cribbage matches, which did a lot to help my mental arithmetical skills; and he introduced me to *Mad* magazine, exotic to me because I had never been permitted comic books.

Most of all we spent hours playing duets. I had taken up French horn along with the various reed instruments, and the two of us played horn duets, free-standing ones and others extracted from classical scores. I was never able to get to the top of the horn register, but happily played second horn to Dick's first, learning alto and tenor harmonization, and learning too the practical value of transposing music at sight from one key to another.

Kek had encouraged this, teaching me to switch between treble and bass clefs, and among the various transpositions in which the music for wind instruments is written: C or "concert," B flat for the clarinets and trumpets and tenor saxophones, E flat for the altos and baritones. This would come in handy a couple of years later, when I went off to college.

Some of us were good enough to participate in the various "clinics" and "honor bands" encouraged in those days, when music was still a significant part of the public-school curriculum. When the city of Richmond built a new civic center, only a block or two from where I'd taken violin lessons ten years before, an honor band was needed to provide one of the concerts. Students from high schools throughout the Bay Area competed for positions, and though I'd only been playing bassoon for a year I took a seat with three other bassoonists in a band that played real music, music written for winds: Handel's *Water Music* and Ralph Vaughan Williams's *English Folk Songs*; I will carry bassoon parts to those scores in my memory, and even in my fingers, until the day I die.

Once I participated in a "select band" drawn from high schools from several northbay counties in an outdoors concert on the Vallejo High School football field. We played a transcription of Strauss's *Death and Transfiguration*, for what reason I will never understand, when a wind came up and scattered our music. The conductor made us start all over again at the beginning, and this time we'd got quite a bit further when a long freight train rumbled past the stadium, quite drowning out the music. We all lost our places but kept playing, and as the train passed and its noise grew less, and our own sounds, completely jumbled, surfaced out of the rumble, the result was quite remarkable — but the conductor stopped us and made us regroup at a recent rehearsal number.

And on one occasion Kek and his wife in the front seat drove three of us band members all the way down to San Diego for a combined honor band and clinic, drawing students from four states. I don't remember the other boy who went; he played trumpet. He may even have been Kek's own son, who I hardly knew; he was immensely popular, an athlete and a class officer of some kind. I certainly remember the girl, LaDonna, who played tenor saxophone, and sat between us in the back seat, much closer to him than to me.

In San Diego I learned that I was not a very good bassoon-ist. I was consigned to the last seat in the section, and I had to fake my way through a number of passages. I also learned what the bassoon was capable of, when at a demonstration desk of some kind I heard a recording of Carl von Weber's *Introduction and Rondo on Hungarian Themes*. I pressed Kek to buy both the record and the sheet music for me, and spent hours trying to master the passagework of this demanding piece, long stretches of which I can still play on the air bassoon, negotiating the amazingly complicated mechanism that Wilhelm Heckel had evolved for the German bassoon a century before, and that was still, mid-20th century, displacing the few French-system instruments still in place in Latin countries.

We also did some touring. I left the country for the first time: we drove across the border into Tijuana, whose utterly exotic streets and crowds were both disturbingly seductive and vaguely disgusting; here I bought a gaudy silver and turquoise bracelet for a girl I'd wanted to get to know, but I never did, and never gave it to her — it remained hidden away from everyone, a secret shameful monument to my growing yearning for romance, and my constant timidity.

We drove around the Salton Sea and marveled at the date palms. We retraced the Highway 101 that I'd traveled a few years earlier with Curt, and I delighted at second sightings of resonant places, the high pass north of San Luis Obispo, the lower one at Paso Robles, the wonderful Missions, the open farm county in the Salinas Valley. And, on the western shore of San Francisco Bay, the prune orchards whose rows of trees fell into changing patterns as we drove by, always a fascinating observation; and the huge blimp hangar at Moffet Field, and at one point a large abandoned building out on the mud flats, where Kek said he'd played in dance bands back during Prohibition, which seemed romantic and illicit to me.

There were other journeys, some of *them* illicit. At least one involved sneaking out to the Russian River and drinking beer and swimming unsupervised; another was with a group of kids to the seashore where we camped overnight and built a huge driftwood bonfire. At least once I skipped school for the day and hitch-hiked down to San Francisco, just to walk the streets and marvel at the buildings. Dick and I were picked up almost immediately by the vice principal of our school, who was driving most of the way on business of some kind; he kindly gave us a lift, but sentenced us to a month of detention beginning the next day. It was worth it. We took streetcars out to Golden Gate Park and to Playland and the Cliff House and Sutro Baths, and best of all we shopped at a music store then on Powell Street, where I bought my first two pocket orchestral scores.

I had discovered by then that the Santa Rosa radio station, KSRO, broadcast an hour of classical music every week, perhaps oftener. I never heard anything more up-to-date than a Strauss tone-poem or a Tchaikovsky symphony, but I listened with fascination to them, trying to imagine the instrumental combinations responsible for the sonorities I heard, and contrasting late Romantic music with the clarity and poise I noticed in the six or eight Haydn symphonies that were occasionally broadcast. So the first scores I bought were Tchaikovsky's *Romeo and Juliet* Overture and Haydn's "Clock" Symphony, the former for its prominent English horn solo (I had fallen in love with that instrument when I finally got my hands on it in High School) and the latter for the prominent bassoon "ticking" of the slow movement.

By then I'd been looking into the scores Mr. Knight conducted from, and I'd been watching his obvious enjoyment as he mediated between their authority and the often labored but always willing performance his band turned in. Kek was left-handed and conducted left-handedly, so it was easy for me to learn the correct right-handed conducting gestures simply by watching him, as Jim had learned upside-down and backward reading and writing by observing me. I didn't do this consciously; it never occurred to me to want to learn to conduct. But it did occur to me that music could be written as well as read, and by then I'd heard a wonderful piece of music on the KSRO concert, vivacious and compelling, and Kek had told me, regretfully, that there was no band transcription of it. So I got hold of some empty manuscript paper with enough lines on it for the entire band and spent hours of free time arranging Schubert's *Rosamunde* Overture for concert band.

After making a rough assignment of parts originally written for the string sections this turned out to be boring work, measure after measure and page after page of repeated notes, and I'm afraid I lost interest toward the end, arbitrarily truncating the piece just where Schubert made his inspired change of tempo to begin the concluding passage. No matter: the parts were never extracted from this arrangement, and I never had any need to finish the self-assignment.

I had also made a band arrangement of the Minuet of Beethoven's Eighth Symphony, which I loved for its horn duet (of course) and exposed clarinet solo. I think this might have been played, except that I could find no logical way of assigning the prominent pizzicato cello line to a band instrument. In the end I gave it to a baritone horn, but no brass-player in our band would have been able to deal with it, so this project too fell by the wayside.

On the other hand I had by then joined two or three other kids in a Dixieland combo, no doubt at Kek's urging. Here I played tuba, and enjoyed our practice sessions — though for some reason we never played in public, so I was never able to prove to my father that I could contribute to music that was completely within his own set of enthusiasms.

Except for conversations of an intellectually speculative kind with Merton, and cribbage and music sessions with Dick, I had virtually no interactions with any of the other kids, either in school or out. For a few weeks I must have attended a church in Sebastopol, for I remember once delivering a short guest sermon from the point of view of a teen-ager, but that didn't last long: I'm sure the inconvenience of my somehow getting there couldn't compete with my lack of real enthusiasm, let alone commitment, to the Christian ideal. I was awkward and very shy, short and unprepossessing until the summer before my senior year, when I grew several inches in three months. I was self-conscious about everything — acne, my clothes, most of all my the stark difference between the world I inhabited with my immediate family — furniture made from automobile seats, home-made bread, cows and pigs in jerrybuilt pens, calves dying of diarrhea, yellowfooted rabbits, filthy ducks, parents who spoke to one another only bitterly or in anger, cars that constantly broke down, no telephone, the squalid bathroom, homemade shirts — everything seemed to make me self-conscious, inadequate, inferior, different. On the school bus and, especially, on the band bus going to football games, I looked at the other kids with a degree of awe and wonder. I knew nothing at all about girls, popular music, dancing, parties; and the only real defense I could mount against all this ignorance and inadequacy was a complete lack of interest in them. If I could not participate, I would not want to.

And then, without my really understanding that the day would inexorably arrive, it was over, and I had graduated from high school. Someone else had to deal with the tenor-clef passage in the "March of the Peers"; I was actually marching, down the aisle, up the stairs, across the stage to take my diploma from the principal.

I was sixteen years old, two months short of my birthday. Harry Truman was in the last year of his presidency. The war in Korea had ended in a draw.

I had attained nearly my full height, six feet; I was skinny, hardly 160 pounds; I was healthy though acne-scarred and already suffering from the bad teeth that ran in my family — and were aggravated by having been only once to see a dentist, and that when I was living with my grandparents. I don't know whether this was because of poverty or some kind of refusal, on Mom's part, to recognize bodily functions and malfunctions. Nearsighted, I was beginning to need glasses for distance, but wore them rarely. After all, I didn't need them for reading.

Emotionally I suppose I was retarded and terribly inner-directed, in the sociological terminology that was just then becoming trendy. I'd been encouraged to resist following any crowd mentality. Mom and Dad encouraged me to accompany them when they visited friends of theirs, the Woods, on a chicken farm two or three miles away. I think this was chiefly because they had a daughter, Loretta, not much younger than me: I have a photo of myself in cap and gown, standing stiffly in a cow-pasture near their egg barn, her at my side: but no friendship grew up between the two of us. I'd had one playmate at Eucalyptus, two good friends at Garfield in Berkeley, and two at high school, all boys. I'd admired a couple of pretty girls at high school — one played E-flat clarinet and lived just south of Sebastopol on our bus route; the other played tenor saxophone and lived north of town on the other end of the route — but I'd never summoned enough self-confidence to talk to them.

Religious instruction had been catch-as-catch-can since returning from Gram and Gramp's, like everything else. There were months when I was some kind of Believer, but I'd never been seized with any degree of enthusiasm. The idea of a Meaning of Life was attractive, and I wouldn't mind some kind of Life After Death, but the idea of innate sin and religious redemption seemed both unpleasant and improbable.

I had no interest in public events. Mom and Dad fought over politics; she was an ardent Republican who had actually approved Roosevelt's death; he was a bluecollar trade-union Democrat who railed against the Taft-Hartley bill that began the erosion of populist politics after the Second World War. This suggested, to me, that any passionately held political opinion was likely simply to be canceled by an opposing one.

My reading had moved beyond children's introductions to mature subjects: Shakespeare, Homer, the Greek myths. I had the Beard history of the United States. I'd been fascinated by lay introductions to math and physics. I'd been introduced to fiction through the family readings aloud from novels — all, I suspect, from the Book-of-the-Month Club, but not from our own subscription, probably titles borrowed from friends and family. I do know that a favorite book was Hendrik Willem van Loon's *Lives*, in which I still read with pleasure from time to time.

In the three years I'd spent at high school, when I was four-teen, fifteen, and sixteen, there'd not been so much exposure to town life. Occasionally, in the summer, I spent a day in Santa Rosa, riding in with Dad in the morning, stashing my lunch in Juilliard Park somewhere, browsing the shops. I loved Sawyer's News Agency; I was already getting interested in paperback ti-tles, and I could look there at *Model Railroader* magazine. I spent time in the stationery stores, admiring papers, rulers, French curves, pens and pencils. And I investigated Hardisty's homewares store with its exotic coffee beans and spices and kitchen equipment. All of this was foreign and mysterious and seductive, but had no place in my own life: I looked at it with-out participating, as one goes to a zoo to wonder at animals whose lives are utterly irrelevant to one's own, however inter-esting and exotic they may be.

Now and then we went to a movie, piling into the car with thermos bottles of coffee and, I suppose, hot chocolate, the six of us, and seeing a Disney movie, or Ma and Pa Kettle, or Francis the Talking Mule at the Redwood Drive-In. But these movies didn't interest me, and as often as not I'd stay home.

There were also occasional drives down to Berkeley, for family gatherings, or just to stay in touch. We'd drive down Or-chard Station Road and the Bodega road to the enticing old road-house at Stony Point, where Dad used to buy shale at the quarry when our driveway needed repair, and then down to Petaluma and Novato where uncle Clay had stopped for his drink, and through San Rafael flying right over town on its sur-prising viaduct, and then out toward San Quentin and the ferry to Richmond. Once we were traveling at night, there must have been some family emergency to cause us to do that, and we missed the last ferry, and had to sleep in the car right there on the road waiting for the first ferry next morning. And at other times the weather would be too bad for the ferries, and we'd go around the other way, on the frightening Black Point road, so foggy you could barely see the pavement, and if you went off it you'd be in the Bay.

I'd been introduced twice to the idea of working for pay. One time Dad drove me to a chicken farm in Cotati, five or six miles away, and I spent a day shoveling manure out from under the cages: I hated it. Another time I worked longer, perhaps two or three weeks, picking berries at a farm adjacent to ours: it was here that I overheard serious and worried talk about the Korean War, and realized I was lucky not to be old enough to be involved. But for the most part I'd spent three years either isolated on a hardscrabble farm, mud or dust, chickens and pigs, increasingly unhappy parents and much younger brothers; or at school, hiding from the other kids in the practice rooms with my beloved woodwinds. Clearly the two things that most appealed to me were music and the countryside, and my parents and grandparents must have been hard put to imagine any kind of professional future for me.

After graduation I spent the summer of 1952 in Berkeley, helping Gramp and his brother Percy and, from time to time, Uncle Bob; they were building what would be the last of the four Crane houses on the east side of Glen Avenue. This one was to be for Gram and Gramp and Barbara and her kids. It seemed immense to me, particularly since it was all on one floor — Gram's mobility had declined to the point she spent most of her time in a wheelchair. It was, I thought, a beautiful house, with a big living-dining room with a cathedral ceiling, and a good-sized kitchen on the east side of the house for the morning light, and a newfangled "family room" next to it with its own fireplace and the piano. Off the hall there were four bedrooms and two bathrooms, and downstairs in the above-ground basement — for the house overlooked a slight drop-off that led across a badly sunlit lawn toward Dorothy and Lester's back yard across the creek — there was a big unfinished room that would be my bedroom when I needed it.

I helped with the shingles and shakes, sheathing the walls and roof of this rambling beauty; and I remember once Gramp shaking his head in disbelief at the dining table, back across the street in the stucco house at 1232 that he would soon be leaving, that a man had looked over the fence from the Rose Garden that afternoon at the new house nearing completion, and had offered fifteen thousand dollars for it, and it not even finished!

During the summer I took a private lesson from a San Francisco Symphony bassoonist, Frank Hibschle, for Kek had allowed me to keep the school bassoon over the summer. I was completely cowed, though, by the discovery that although my proficiency had taken me as far as San Diego, in fact I knew virtually nothing about the complexities of the instrument — even had used the wrong fingering all those years for one of the most frequently played notes. On the other hand, I enjoyed visiting him backstage during a performance at a summer Pops concert of the Saint-Saëns "Organ" symphony — he was sitting it out, as it had no contrabassoon part. We spoke quietly, and now and then the organ would drown out our whispers, and he'd denounce "that awful machine." (I was entranced with another piece on the program, George Enesco's *First Romanian Rhapsody*, finding it savage and dramatic.)

And then it was August, and I celebrated my seventeenth birthday, and got in the car with Mom and Dad and a couple of suitcases, and rode back down Highway 101 to Los Angeles, where my grandparents had decided I would attend a small church-run boarding college for at least a year, and begin some kind of transition out of childhood, and try out two alternative courses, one preparing for a successful and influential life in the ministry, the other the clearly impractical and demanding field of music instruction — alternatives suggested by an "aptitude test" that I'd taken, whether routinely at Analy High or especially through some other agency I don't remember.

On the drive to Los Angeles we stopped for the night at a cheap motel in Carpinteria, a few miles downcoast from Santa Barbara. After dinner Mom suggested going for a walk, "to stretch our legs." We walked silently, she and I; the night was warm and dark, with a cool breeze off the noisy sea. She puffed on her inevitable cigarette, finally speaking only one sentence: "Just don't let one of those floozies get you." I turned the advice over silently in my mind, at a loss as to how to respond, other than an automatic assurance that I wouldn't. What was a floozie, exactly; how should I evade one; what would she do with me once she'd "got" me?

Summer of 1952

5: Los Angeles and back, 1952-1955

CHAPMAN COLLEGE WAS A CLUSTER of brick buildings occupying an entire block on the east side of Vermont Avenue, a little north of the Hollywood Freeway then under construction. Three buildings formed a quadrangle whose fourth side was open to a parking lot fronting Vermont: library and classrooms; chapel and social hall; and dormitory. The dorm was a fourstorey building, long and rather narrow, with bedrooms arranged alongside a narrow corridor. There were two of these arrangements, in fact, one for boys, one for girls, as if a secure wall had been thrust through the building, lengthwise, basement to top, to separate the sexes.

I shared a room for a short time, occupying a top bunk, but soon enough was assigned a single room: single bed, small table and two chairs, small bookcase, sink. Bathing and toilet facilities may have been shared with an adjacent bedroom, or may have been shared by the entire floor, I no longer remember.

Chapman College, in addition to being private and small and religious, was distinguished by offering its classes on a novel schedule, whose experimental nature may have helped persuade Mom that it was a good choice for me. The "solid" courses, history and literature and language and science, were given intensively, three hours a morning, five days a week, for six weeks. Then you'd take the final exam, and go on to the next subject. The only exceptions to this were physical education and music performance, which occupied the afternoons.

My first job, after getting a room assignment and orienting myself to the dining hall and library, was to register for classes. The first one was required: a survey class in the psychology of religion. This was taught earnestly and, I believe, rather well; the two texts were a history of religion, by one Ebenezer Pratt, and William James's *The Varieties of Religious Experience*. Of the course I remember only being fascinated with the *Varieties*, and the definition of religion given by the other text: "Religion is the serious and social attitude toward that which is conceived as controlling one's destiny." I've given that definition a good deal of thought in the last half-century; it seems a good one to me, as the concept of control seems central to the psychological sources, urges, and uses of religion, both individually and politically, revealing much of the power of this complex force.

At the time, though, this course was primarily interesting for its introduction, to me at least, of psychology, a subject I'd never really thought about until then. It was interesting, too, for the dynamics of its procedure: twenty or so students, none apparently known to one another, all listening to what was clearly a carefully prepared lecture, reading the text outside of class, looking up assigned further reading in the library, discussing various points and asking for further explanations of subtleties and complexities.

In the afternoon a few of us were driven, I don't recall how, up to Griffith Park, at the end of Vermont Avenue, to the tennis courts, for I'd chosen what seemed the most individual of sports from the short list of athletic options on that registration day. Here we were nevertheless lined up as a group, and taught to toss a tennis ball straight up, using our left hand, and to catch it, and repeat the toss, over and over. We were taught to serve before we were taught to rally. Before long, though, we were actually playing, always doubles games.

Across the street from the college there were a few wooden "temporary" classroom buildings, no doubt built just after the war, and here I took my second six-week course, an introduction to harmony. It was the first serious class in music theory I'd ever taken, given my a round, pink-faced, fresh-scrubbed Englishman, Dr. Sholund. There were eight students, only two of whom, he once said in a fit of exasperation, showed much promise; I liked to think that he glanced at me at the moment and included me in the two.

He must have been an excellent teacher, for he soon had us singing four-part chorales at sight, and taking dictation — he'd play a melodic line at the piano and we were to write it out with pencil and paper. He assigned short phrases from real compositions for us to analyze harmonically, and I remember the final examination, which required us to identify, then analyze several measures of orchestral music, then write a new piece of music using the same harmonic structure but a melody of our own devising. (Only one other student identified the source, a cadential passage from the first movement of the Schumann piano concerto.)

Piano was obligatory to any student who took a music course like this, so I had signed up for five practice periods and an individual lesson each week. My old practice habits interfered with any success at the keyboard, though. I hated the sharp keys I was made to practice; scales and arpeggios bored me; and I spent nearly all my practice time improvising melodies and exploring further the fascinating harmonic progressions I was studying.

I had more fun in orchestra, though I was badly disappointed at having to give up the bassoon. The college didn't own one, and of course my family had never given any thought to buying me one; the expense was unthinkable. Nor had anyone suggested that I might have earned the money myself: cleaning out a chickenhouse and picking blackberries weren't much of a start..

In any case there was no bassoon, but the orchestra, such as it was, was preparing its first concert, and one of the pieces, Ippolitov-Ivanov's *Caucasian Sketches*, had some prominent bassoon solos. I was playing French horn, but managed to play a few measures of the bassoon part as well, during rests in my own part. This earned a pleasant compliment from the conductor, who I otherwise do not remember: but when time came to play the concert, "ringers" were brought in from outside to sit in on bassoon and even French horn, and I was given the triangle to play — still a prominent role, and one that pleased me, and taught me that no instrument is an easy one to play musically, and no instrument is too modest to be given a position of importance.

Little by little I began to explore the city around me, but always timidly. First I found a record store just across the street from the college. It was small but had a good selection of inexpensive records on the cut-rate Remington label, and I bought what I could with my meager allowance. I spent hours there, listening to records in the listening booth, talking about music with the proprietor, a short, stocky man who always wore a grey sweatshirt, and who seemed bland and timid like myself, a naive man I see now who tried to sell a song he'd written to the Chopin Prelude in A, taking his inspiration from the "Evening Concert" broadcast every night by a local radio station:

> *An evening concert, dear,*
> *Whenever you are near...*

There was another customer who spent a half-hour or so every day like me, listening and conversing, an older man, always neatly dressed in jacket and necktie. He knew an impressive amount about music and recordings, and bought two or three new records every day: but one day I realized I hadn't seen him for a week or so, and asked about him, and was told, mournfully, that he'd skipped town, no one knew where he'd gone, and he owed the record store several hundred dollars.

Beyond the record store, up Vermont Avenue, there was a lunch restaurant of sorts with picnic tables set out under an enormous pepperwood tree; and beyond that a shabby grocery store where I got into trouble one day; I pocketed a small package of cheese and was apprehended at the door by the owner, who threatened to have me arrested and made me swear never to return to his store. This ended my criminal experiment, and a good thing too; I had no aptitude for it.

I was however becoming troublesome, and troubled. For one thing, the floozy had arrived, and fascinated me, and taught me shared pleasures I hadn't really understood until then — stolen kisses and, one warm night, experimental gropings that went further. This was a difficult relationship to pursue on the campus of a private boarding school of religious bent, but we did what we could, and more than once had to be reminded of the rule in the social hall: mixed-sex couples could not sit so close together that another person couldn't sit down between them.

I had also begun to smoke. It seemed to me that a college man should smoke a pipe, and one day I'd taken a walk down Santa Monica Boulevard as far as Sears, Roebuck — a store with which I was familiar — and there I'd bought myself a bent-stem pipe, and somewhere else a package of Prince Albert tobacco, and in the privacy, as I thought, of my room I learned to deal with pipe, tobacco, package, matches, and all that. And from there it wasn't much of a step to drinking: an older student, a fascinating young man with a glass eye and a Finnish name, who reputedly had once arranged music for the Les Brown dance-band, had a fondness for white wine, and shared squat green bottles of Chilean Riesling with me, and occasionally a Rheingau; I remember we used to get a 1947 black-label Rheingau that was golden and fragrant, and cost less than a dollar a bottle.

Before long I was drinking gin and bitters. I must have read about this in one of those old *Esquire* magazines, years earlier; I can't imagine anyone else drinking that combination, even in 1952 or '53. And I hung a dart board on my side of the door to my room, and was selling drinks to other students from a bar improvised across my sink: but one day the door was opened without a knock, and the dean of students was standing there disapprovingly, and I was ejected from the dormitory.

I don't know how I broke the news to my parents, or they to my grandparents; or what this may have represented financially to them. I continued to take classes, but didn't finish the year. I found a room soon enough, though, in a small bungalow owned by a dour single woman of indeterminate age who wore a dark wig and worked at some office job and listened in her spare time to Wagner operas on 78 rpm records, two or three minutes on a side, making up as complete a performance as possible by cutting back and forth between various labels, and giving me a distaste for Wagner I've never been able to overcome.

I shared my room with a young man who was a student at the nearby Los Angeles City College, whose campus was on Vermont across from the record store. His name was Fikret, he was a Turk and a Mohammedan, and we had little in common. Before long, wanting something more private, I found another room in a large, vaguely Victorian house set back from the street. It was owned by a couple with a small daughter; they eked out the husband's salary as a postal clerk by renting out rooms. His wife, Anna, was an intriguing cook; she once left a roast of beef to marinate for a day or two in onions and red wine in a shady spot on the screened-in back porch, and the result, once cooked, was cut into tiny pieces and eaten like candy. It was delicious. And the husband, whose name I cannot remember, read aloud to us all but especially to his daughter from a book I'd never heard of, *Finnegans Wake*, long paragraphs that were perfectly incomprehensible to me, but melodic and somehow funny.

He introduced me to a friend, Herb Alf, who had a house not too far away on what seemed a huge lot, on the crown of a hill; and Herb hired me to help him fence the property. He had a fascinating way of doing this: he bought large expanses of some kind of steel mesh, and I cut these into sections which we rolled up and set into fence-posts we'd dug, and then we wired pairs of mesh panels between the posts, and filled posts and panels with concrete we mixed by hand. It was hard work but pleasant, out of doors under the warm Los Angeles sky, grey with smog more often than blue but more pleasant than the classroom, not to mention the dormitory room; and before long I gave no thought whatever to school, and simply stopped going.

I enjoyed the small-town feel of my little corner of Los Angeles. There was a Greek restaurant near Santa Monica and Vermont, where I used to enjoy a big bowl of salad with croutons and feta — how sophisticated I felt! A block or two west, on Santa Monica Boulevard, there were two or three miniature golf courses, and I often played, solo of course for lack of friends. There were tall palms lining the streets, and plenty of sun, and relative quiet; I don't think the neighborhood was much noisier than Blank Road had been, and there were no chores to do.

Herb's money only held out so long, though, and before long I had to find other ways of supporting myself, as I'd cut myself completely away from home by then. I worked for a while as a stevedore of some kind on the railroad, taking the bus over to the yards out near Chinatown, where I worked loading and unloading freight from boxcars. I worked for a while as a cook at a hamburger joint at Santa Monica and Vermont, where I peeled potatoes and sliced them and blanched them in boiling water, then cooled them by plunging them into buckets of ice-water where they remained, ready to be deep-fried on order.

I answered a job interview one day at a local hospital, the Cedars of Lebanon: the job advertised was that of an orderly, but the employment officer sensed that I had intellectual potential beyond that, and put me in a training position in the office.

Here I soon became a Night Auditor, spending the hours from midnight until eight o'clock going over the previous day's postings of payments, finding any discrepancies and tracking down errors in posting and billing. This seemed Important at first, and I sat at the desk in a green eyeshade, smoking my pipe, and looking for transposed figures, totaling up the columns on a ten-key adding machine. But before long that job too was boring, and when I relieved my boredom one night by striding around the office roaring like a lion I was relieved also of my duties.

I was apparently not quite in my right mind. For one thing, I had determined to get married. After a month or two with the Wagner-lover and the Turk, and another month or two listening to *Finnegans Wake*, I decided it was time for me to preside over my own establishment, to take out my own garbage, to make a household. The girl was, of course, the first one I'd met at Chapman; she had well and truly got hold of me. When I turned eighteen — she was a year or so older than I was — we could legally marry without parental permission, so we convinced Mom and Dad that it was futile to withhold it. She was a Richmond girl; perhaps I'd even known her in the second grade — we'd gone to the same school. To make the marriage even more inevitable, her father played French horn, in the community band. They lived in a very ordinary stucco bungalow filled with middle-class collectibles; they attended a neighborhood Protestant church of some kind; I'm sure they seemed safe enough to my family, and perhaps our families thought this quick embrace of domesticity would provide the incentive I needed to buckle down, finish school, get a teaching degree, and settle down.

So one day when I was visiting the Bay Area, probably getting to know her parents but crashing with Gram and Gramp for a few days, Mom and Dad dropped me off at Albany Hospital, where I gave the required blood sample to prove I was not syphilitic, and at an office somewhere to get the marriage license. And a few weeks later, just short of my eighteenth birthday, we had a nice conventional wedding, white gown and all, in a church in Richmond, and then we somehow got back to Los Angeles and took up married life in a small apartment on North New Hampshire Street, a few blocks from Chapman College.

It was a studio apartment, with a small kitchen alcove, and a desk, and a Murphy bed that folded down from the wall. I worked, when I did, either at the hospital or at the hamburger shack, I no longer remember the sequence of events, and she worked at the telephone company up on Vermont Avenue. And I continued to think about music, though I had no instrument other than a small portable phonograph. The previous winter I'd seen my first opera, a production of *La fille du régiment* that San Francisco Opera had brought on the annual Los Angeles tour they made in those days; Gram had arranged for me to have a free ticket, as a church friend of theirs, Ernest Lawrence, was singing the male lead across Lily Pons in the title role. And I had also seen film versions of operas, *The Tales of Hoffmann* and *Il barbiere di Siviglia*, along with *The Red Shoes*; and the power of musical theater had got hold of me far beyond my realization; that was the floozy Mom had better have warned me about.

The warnings and disapprovals my love life had met gave me my theme. Back at Chapman College the other students had whispered about us, I was convinced; and the authorities had disapproved (and in fact that may have been behind my ejection from the dormitory); and our families had tried to stop us. Taking a cue from Rossini's opera I decided that *Slander's Whispers* would make a fine title for an opera about true love surviving social disapproval, but I never got much further than the title.

I spent more time on another idea. At Chapman my only real male friend was a violin student, also named Charles, and he had demonstrated the whole-tone scales to me one day; I

had no idea that such nonstandard things existed. I was fascinated, and decided to write an entire violin concerto in the
whole-tone scale; the opening is still in my mind:

But, as had been the case with Schubert's *Rosamunde* Overture, the sheer drudgery of writing all those eighth-notes, combined with the utter unlikelihood of the result ever being
played, discouraged me from finishing the piece.

I'd seen *La fille du régiment*, and I'd been to one concert by
the Los Angeles Philharmonic, which played in those days in a
Foursquare Gospel temple in one of the many dirty squat brick
office-buildings downtown — I remember only that the experience was stuffy and uninteresting. I heard the college madrigal
singers once or twice:

> *Sing we and chaunt it*
> *While love doth graunt it*
> *Tra la la la la…*

It is permanently etched in my mind's ear, along with
some mildly risqué catches and glees by Purcell and his con-
temporaries (not performed, to be sure, on campus). Otherwise
I don't think I heard any live music.

I was adding to my record collection, already concentrating
on pieces on the edge of the conventional concert repertory
rather than the war-horses. I preferred Liszt to Beethoven,
tone-poems to abstract music. I was drawn to music that was
colorful and attempted some kind of musical depiction, rather
than abstract concert music; and I liked the tone-colors of exotic instruments and full orchestras, not piano solos or chamber
music. On one foray down into Hollywood I'd found a shop
that sold orchestral scores, among them Enesco's *First Romanian Rhapsody*, the one I'd heard the summer before in San
Francisco; and I listened to a little ten-inch LP of that piece,

following the score, many times, hopelessly trying to teach myself by osmosis to compose like that.

I had no real idea how to engage the actual substance of music; I'm not sure I realized there was such a thing. I was infatuated with the qualities of life, but unaware of its substance. Someone told me, for example — perhaps the one-eyed dance-band arranger, perhaps the record-store proprietor — that there was a place on Vine Street where Stravinsky took his manuscripts to be copied for publication, and I went there and got a price list, and gazed uncomprehendingly at a Stravinsky manuscript page framed and hanging on the office wall. I sat in Coffee Dan's, next door, and had coffee and a slice of blueberry pie, spending fifteen cents I could ill afford. I walked: bus fare was better spent on other things, and while I knew how to drive — Dad had taught me years earlier, and anyway Driving Instruction was a required course at Analy High — actually *having* a car was well beyond me.

Before I turned eighteen, in August 1953, I had to register for the draft, and escaping any future war, or even the temporary interruption of peacetime service for three years, seemed a matter of some urgency. Someone suggested a strategy: I found the draft board that served a part of town that produced very few college students and registered there, immediately drawing a student deferment. In the next few years I was to change residence several times, rarely providing the draft board with the new address, and after a while I suppose the draft board lost interest in me, and so I avoided service. I think this is unfortunate: the discipline of boot camp and the steady employment of a three-year hitch would have made an entirely different man of me; and in any case Korea was over, and Vietnam too far in the future, to have involved me. But this is speculation.

I have, oddly, no memory at all of our domestic life; the only image that comes to mind of that New Hampshire Street apartment is the little portable phonograph and the box of long-playing records. But domestic life couldn't have been very rewarding, for either of us, and word must have got back to Berkeley and Blank Road of my failure to contribute anything to it of a pecuniary nature. And so one day early in 1954 Mom and Dad appeared at the front door: they'd borrowed a station wagon from someone, and loaded up our few belongings, and we drove silently north, my wife next to me in the back seat, Mom and Dad typically silent up front. We drove, for some reason, by way of the tank farm and the Carquinez Bridge: were the ferries not running? And in one day, it seems, we arrived at the brokendown farm on Blank Road, from which, in a matter of days, my wife would leave, never to be seen again by any of us.

I doubt that I had ever really engaged with her, any more than I had ever engaged with anyone, with any subject. The world consisted of nothing but sensory impressions and a few apparently invariable natural laws. One could evade difficulties — anger, unpredicted emotions, violence — by simply failing to attend to them. I would learn later that the Japanese had a term for this, the "floating world." In the early 1950s there was no drug culture, at least not in the world I knew, other than alcohol of course; had there been I might well have embraced it at that point.

For a week or so she somehow stuck it out. We had one of the bedrooms, and my three little brothers, the oldest of them only thirteen, looked on our relationship, our addition to their own cluttered and troubled household, as just one more imponderable in the irrational domestic life that was theirs, and Dad drove into Santa Rosa to work, and Mom silently stared out the windows at night, and the chickens and the rabbits and the pigs made their usual demands. Dick and Merton, my two friends from Analy, had been attendants at our wedding, and though Merton had gone off to college somewhere Dick was still around, and the three of us would occasionally go out for a drive; my wife had loved riding the buses when she was in high school, there was nothing she liked better, it seemed, than riding around, particularly riding fast down steep hills, and one day Dick failed to make a right-angled turn on a country road at the bottom of a hill, out near Loretta's chicken ranch, and the car spun around and crashed backwards into a fencepost. I remember that the Mendelssohn violin concerto was playing on the radio, and that I thought Damn, I'm going to die and won't hear the end of this piece: but of course we didn't die; we helped ourselves out of the car and walked to a neighboring farmhouse and somehow got a ride home, and Dick's car wasn't seriously injured, no more than were we.

But soon enough, I'm not sure how, my wife realized that nothing good would ever come of any of this, and she left. Mom must have had conversations with her, and no doubt there were some negotiations of some kind between her and my parents, and involving her parents as well, and Gram and Gramp; but I remember no involvement at all, of any kind, in any such discussions, or in any part of the separation. And that spring, the spring of 1954, I enrolled in courses at Santa Rosa Junior College, where this most difficult period of my life would reach its first nearly fatal climax.

Soon enough I met another girl, a fascinating one I thought, dark and wilful and apparently with a mental and emotional life of her own, one that had an existence completely apart from any moments she shared with me. I was not used to contending with something like this, and the very reality of her having a life apart from mine, and the necessity of intruding on that life from time to time, was a fascinating challenge. Her parents lived in Albany, not far as it turned out from Albany Hospital, a landmark for me since it was there I'd had that blood test, and once or twice I drove here there; by now I had a car of my own, Dad had bought a 1933 Plymouth for me, cautioning me never to drive it over forty miles an hour lest it blow its engine. Charlotte also had a dog, a German shepherd, or at least on one occasion we had such a dog with us, and when I was pulled over by a cop in Petaluma for not stopping quite decisively enough at a red light the dog actually bit him when he was unprofessional enough to reach into the back seat to pet him, and I got my first traffic ticket.

I called the Plymouth Rocinante. It was painted a soft baby blue, and had mohair headlining and seats. It lacked a radiator cap, and I turned an evaporated-milk can upside down over the filler and drove it that way for months. There was something wrong with the generator and the battery was often run down, but it had a crank that I could start it with, and at night I could coast when I needed the headlights, then turn off the head-lights when I needed the engine. I drove it as far as Berkeley once, to park romantically up in the bills; and for other roman-tic excursions out into the fields along Bennett Valley Road, out south of Santa Rosa.

For the first time I was really in love, I thought; in love with a real woman, with a life and interests of her own — my poor wife had always been some kind of trophy or symbol of domesticity; it had never occurred to me to investigate anything of real substance in her own life, nor did she ever volunteer any enthusiasm or interest beyond fast rides on country roads, or singing in the oddly assorted madrigal group at Chapman, or, oddest of all (and most intriguing, if I'd only had the wits to re-alize it and follow up on it), a large fullsize reproduction of a disturbing painting by Yves Tanguy that she'd admired in a framing-shop window, and that I'd bought for her, and that hung for a time on the living room wall at Blank Road.

But Charlotte was equally interested in another boy, one who undoubtedly had his act better together. And one who played piano, and played well, considerably better than I'd ever be able to. And who improvised on it in the manner of Rach-maninoff, stormy dark rhapsodic stuff that was all emotion, I suddenly realized, and no real musical depth; and I looked on helplessly as she came to prefer that stuff, and to be bored by my neurotic expostulations; and one day, in her car, not mine, she told me she never wanted to see me again, and there was nothing I could do. I remember kissing her, kissing a face that had no life behind it.

There was nothing to do but play music. Santa Rosa Junior College had a small but rather interesting music department. There weren't enough students who played stringed instruments to make up an orchestra, but there was a small concert band of sorts, and there was an instrument-locker room with a couple of French horns to spare, and a tuba, and even a bassoon — though the bassoon was assigned to an older student who'd been there the year before, and was only available to me from time to time.

Dick was there, too, and he and I began investigating wind chamber-music more closely. It was here that we found the Mozart horn concertos, and the Reicha wind quintets; and while there was virtually never anyone else to play oboe and clarinet and flute we played our way through many of those quintets, imagining the missing instruments. Here too I arranged a Bach fugue, the little g minor one, for Dixieland quartet, trumpet and clarinet and trombone and tuba, and actually heard the result in the practice room one day, Dick playing the trombone part on the French horn, me on the tuba, and two other kids, nonplussed I'm sure, on the other two lines.

There was a community orchestra, whose sole purpose was apparently the annual performance of Handel's *Messiah* at Christmastime. That first winter I played second horn in the performance, always ready to cover for the first horn in case its player, who taught the band instruments at SRJC, was too inattentive for whatever reason to recognize his cue. Dick was unavailable to play that year, for some reason; or perhaps I have the winters mixed up, and it was that first winter that I played kettledrums, and Dick played second horn.

Dick was a constant companion; I'm sure I'd have lost my mind entirely if it hadn't been for his sympathy and attentiveness. We played horn together; we played cribbage; we talked about *Mad* magazine. We went for drives; he was very good about ferrying me here and there. Once his sensitive hearing saved us when, had I been driving, we would surely have been killed: in those days there were frequent dense tule fogs hovering over the plains south and west of Santa Rosa, and we were driving slowly at night, blinded by our headlights reflecting back at us on a night too dark to drive without them, when he suddenly stopped. We got out and walked forward a few feet; he was sure he'd heard something. Suddenly we saw a freight train barreling across Todd Road, southbound for Petaluma. Another few feet and we'd have driven into it.

By now I was without a car of my own. I'd damaged the Plymouth's steering somehow to the extent that it couldn't negotiate a normal right turn; you had to plan your course carefully and compensate with many left turns. The reverse gear was gone, too, which made parallel parking difficult. And eventually Dad had taken it over, to fix it up he said, but before he could he drove it in front of a hay truck one drunken night, and while he emerged unhurt the poor Plymouth was demolished.

But while Dick was loyal and generous with me he too fell in love, with a big bright challenging girl named Arlyn, and the attention he'd formerly lavished on me was now shared with her. A number of times I went out to her home, in the Bennett Valley foothills east of Santa Rosa, now covered with tract houses but then quite open grazing land. There the two young lovers would cuddle quietly for hours on a big overstuffed armchair while I conversed with Arlyn's mother Gwen, whose literacy and life experience I found more interesting than Arlyn's youthful pulchritude.

There were other acquaintances, of course. One of them, a soft-spoken graceful brunette with a pleasant North Carolina drawl, was probably more interested in me than I was in her. She visited once or twice out on Blank Road, once revealing she was a crack shot with a .22 rifle, another time bringing a handsome and friendly exchange student from Nigeria to a sort of work party Dad suggested I arrange, ostensibly to make some repairs to our unpaved driveway — more likely, as I think about it, because he and Mom were genuinely concerned about my increasing withdrawal into myself.

And then, somehow, I met Carma. There was a semester, either that fall or the following spring, the spring of 1955, when I was taking French and English literature and a psychology course, and met two girls who opened my eyes and my mind onto a world of ideas and issues quite beyond any I'd earlier known: one of them was Carma, the other was Gaye: two names fraught with symbolism: fate and joy.

Of the two it was Carma who was moodier, the more enigmatic, and of course I fell completely in love with her. She lived in a little basement apartment in Santa Rosa, and I spent long hours there with her listening to music. We used to listen to the Gershwin piano concerto which I introduced her to, and the Khatchaturian piano concerto which she introduced me to, and, oddest of all I thought, a recording she loved and taught me to appreciate, a collection of mood pieces called *Music for Barefoot Ballerinas*; and she even tried to get me to listen to Gordon Jenkins's *Manhattan Towers*, but I wouldn't have anything of such sentiment.

She had a fiancé of sorts, a fellow named Norman, but he was away in the army, and she was lonely. And she had another admirer, a dangerously intense fellow named Jerry, who drove an imported car and read Hemingway and loved depictions of violence, and who once entered unannounced and found us in bed together — we used to snuggle chastely to keep warm while listening to music; it was, unfortunately for me, nothing more serious than that, but he could hardly have known, and he pointed his .45 caliber Colt revolver at us, he used to go target-shooting with it, and I thought quickly if ungallantly and drew her over between me and the gun, and she talked him into a degree of calmness.

By now I had left Blank Road. It had got harder and harder to get home by daylight; one final night I barely made it, running much of the way —- the years of track at Analy had been good for me — and I realized the futility and probably the hypocrisy of the attempt. Mom probably knew what was going on, but she never said a word about it. Dad must have known, and was probably amused; but his own delinquencies were making any opinion of his quite irrelevant to my own view of things. So one night I just stayed at Carma's, and the next day I got a job flipping hamburgers at the delightfully named Eat'n'Run, an early experiment in drive-up fast food; and found a furnished room in a gathering of shacks on the banks of Santa Rosa Creek, right in town.

By now I was acting pretty crazy, though I was able to hold a job, with the sympathy and patience of the man who ran the Eat'n'Run. I was still very thin, my hands were shaky, I habitually wore various permutations of two worsted suits I had inherited from my great-uncle Clarence, Gramp's brother, a man who was four inches shorter and forty pounds heavier than I. I wore a sparse beard and a wool beret — Gramp had always worn one, so it seemed not entirely an affectation — and I mumbled, self-conscious about my bad teeth, another two of which had recently been pulled.

I hardly socialized at all, but there were exceptions. I was persuaded to join the French Club, and I think I was indulged a bit by the French teacher, Mrs. Godkin, who tried to get me to approach language with some discipline but readily gave in to my usual approach, trying to absorb it by simply exposing myself to it. In addition to French I took a course in French literature, reading Prevost and Balzac and Gide, and I joined a literary club, and with Gaye and Carma and her pistol-packing boy friend submitted stories and poems to the campus literary magazine, *First Leaves*.

I continued in the community orchestra, switching to kettledrums for the next *Messiah* and, more satisfyingly for its exposed kettledrum solo, Beethoven's Mass in C. And by then I was writing a little music. I'd abandoned the violin concerto long since, and under the influence of a favorite recording, Mitch Miller's performance of the Vaughan Williams Oboe Concerto, had begun a double concerto for oboe, horn, and strings. Before getting too far in that, and realizing that I had to come to terms with smaller forces, I wrote the first movement of a string quartet, much influenced by the sound, though not the technique, of the Debussy quartet. I was still unfamiliar with any newer music, though I'd befriended a small, shy boy, Joe Halpin, who played piano, and who lived in a shabby old-fashioned bungalow on the margin of Santa Rosa's business district — and who had, surprisingly when I look back on it, corresponded with the famously reclusive American composer Charles Ives, who had sent a large box of photostat scores to him: I remember Joe showing me the Fourth Symphony. Although I couldn't take it in intellectually, it immediately burned itself into my imagination, and would profoundly influence me later.

Music, though, was giving way to literature as a dominating enthusiasm. I drew considerable praise from my first English teacher since the ninth grade, drawing top grades in first-semester English, and qualifying to skip the required second semester and go directly to more critical classes. There was a brilliant if immensely modest man teaching literature at SRJC, Sidney Meller: he introduced me to the Novel and to the hitherto unsuspected critical niceties by which one could study the novel as an art form beyond its simple narrative. Until then fiction, like music and for that matter the people I met in life, was no more than the surface it presented when I was engaged with it; now it began to reveal the substance of its independent reality.

Through these courses in the novel I was learning, though I didn't realize it at the time, that literature, and therefore probably music, and even the people I met and dealt with had hidden structural techniques and even significances, hidden behind the various facades they presented on first reading or

hearing or meeting, sometimes conflicting with or even contra-
dicting their immediate apparent meaning, and often held in
various ways in common. You could classify these individual
books and compositions and people as to type, for example.
Even something as apparently dry and rigid as musical form —
sonata-allegro, ABA song, rondo — could be studied for its in-
teraction with something as fluid and dynamic as the sounds to
whose unfolding delights it lent some kind of esthetic coherence.

But coherence was not yet the uppermost value of my approach to daily experience. I was infatuated with music, literature, conversation of a sort; I was hungry for tastes and experiences. It was an insanely lyrical moment. In my little room I
read constantly in an anthology of medieval Persian poetry, not
for the narratives — I doubt I ever read a long poem all the way
through — but for the imagery. I read a good deal of science
fiction, again most often stories, not full-length books.

On the other hand, encouraged by Meller, I was reading
novels — Mark Twain, Hemingway, Faulkner, Fitzgerald, Stephen Crane, early Henry James, Robert Nathan's *One More
Spring* that so beautifully paraphrased my own lyrical optimism
in the face of poverty. We read also Tolstoy and Dostoevsky
and Virginia Woolf and, best of all, Joyce; and having been exposed to *Finnegans Wake* a year or two before I was introduced
to *A Portrait of the Artist as a Young Man*, whose title character
seemed an uncanny embodiment of my own pretensions and
anxieties and sensitivities; I could easily forgive Stephen Deda-
lus his so much better education than my own.

I had met an older man, Jack McLean, who took a few
courses at SRJC between long periods away during which he
worked sorting mail on railroad cars traveling up and down
California's central valley. Jack had requested the Santa Rosa
library acquire a copy of *Finnegans Wake*, an inspired request it
seemed to me; I hadn't before realized that one could impose
one's own desire on the system to that extent, and had thought

of libraries, like the radio, as essentially to be used passively, being grateful for whatever interesting matter they might provide. This had in fact been my orientation to virtually every corner of experience: I was utterly passive, yet resistant to external direction. But I spent long hours in conversation with Jack, sometimes in the JC student union, sometimes at the home of an older woman, a friend of his, who lived in a cabin in the redwoods near Monte Rio; and I began at his suggestion to keep a journal in a spiral-bound notebook with blue-ruled pages on which I recorded little fragments of verse or imagined conversations. The cover of the notebook was cheap cardboard, and on it I wrote in my most flourished of script a punning title: *Satyrday Review of Literature*. (I wasn't yet clever enough to spell the final word with a double "t.") It was apparently not individual contents, but the superficial and immediate sense of their accumulation, that was important to me, had I only had the objectivity to see it.

I was buying books by then, whatever paperbacks I could afford. It was my eighteenth year, the winter of 1953 and spring of 1954, the beginning of a sort of general cultural reawakening in the United States following what seemed the national introspection of the second Truman administration. There were foreign movies to be seen: a Finnish one, about a witch who ran free, naked, among the birches, was spoken of with some wonder and excitement in the Junior College cafeteria. And Sawyer's News Agency was selling the then-new lines of paperback books, New American Classics and Mentor Books, making Faulkner and Joyce as readily available as Hemingway and Steinbeck; and offering non-fiction by George Gamow and Ruth Benedict and Margaret Mead as well; and, most excitingly as far as I was concerned, serial anthologies like *New World Writing* devoted to contemporary literature.

The only thing missing, so completely missing that I didn't realize it was missing, was the avant garde. I had spent two years in Los Angeles, and had studied a little music with an intelligent and no doubt sophisticated teacher, but had never heard of Schoenberg who had died there only the year before. I knew Stravinsky was somehow present but had no idea his music could actually be heard. Chapman College was within easy walking distance of the famous salon Peter Yates was keeping in the celebrated rooftop music room of his home, but I never knew about it.

Santa Rosa seemed to have no salon at all; at least I never heard of one. The closest things, for me, were meetings of our literary club in Mr. Meller's snug bungalow on Humboldt Street, where we had tea and cakes and possibly even sherry along with our conversation, and the occasional meetings of the French Club, where Mrs. Godkin encouraged us to reveal our various stages of intellectual growth in little show-and-tells. One day, for example, I showed a little still-life I had painted using leftover tubes of oils Mom had kept for twenty years from her Carmel days, and using a stick and a palette knife but no brush, because I had none. It was not the content of the painting but the technique that had interested me, the technique and the heavy impasto and obsessively repeated patterns of raised details that resulted.

One of these meetings was in someone's home on a rainy day: the grey drab mood of the weather and my own lyrical pessimism inspired me to improvise a little song at the piano, and my first finished composition resulted, a setting of one of Joyce's lyrics from *Chamber Music*:

> *Rain has fallen all the day*
> *O come among the laden trees:*
> *The leaves lie thick upon the way*
> *Of memories...*

I was sufficiently neurotic by now to have alarmed either my parents or the authorities at SRJC, or possibly both, and I was seeing the school-appointed psychologist, first in his office, soon enough more informally in the living room of his modest cottage out on Stony Point Road. Dr Ross was a friendly, quiet, intelligent man whose own interpretation of whatever ailed me never really seemed to be an important part of our conversations: perhaps it was reserved for my parents or the authorities. He began, at an early meeting, by assessing my intelligence and the physical state of my nervous system: I put together puzzles in two dimensions and in three, and took Rorschach tests and random-association tests, and engaged in conversation.

This quickly drifted to a relationship that seemed primarily social — not really a friendship; the origin of the relationship was too recent to allow me to make that mistake; and then there was a kind of distance between us that I didn't feel, for example, with my older friend Jack, or even with Mrs. Godkin or Mr. Meller. Perhaps it was simply Dr. Ross's way of examining my mental and emotional interactions more closely and in situations more similar to daily experience. In any case he introduced me to his young nephew, with whom I went once or twice on swimming expeditions to the beach on the Russian River, in Healdsburg, fifteen miles north; lying in the sun, he said, would be good for my acne-scarred complexion.

And in Dr. Ross's living room we listened to the 78 rpm recordings of Virgil Thomson's *Four Saints in Three Acts*, which joined *Finnegans Wake* in my introduction to the avant garde.

¶ ¶ ¶

And so passed the first half of 1954, first with my family on Blank Road, then in Santa Rosa, attending classes and working. I remember that for Christmas my parents had given me a suede jacket, what we called in those days a bomber-style jacket, zipping up the front; and that on an exceptional day Dick and I had driven up Mt. St. Helena, an hour or so away, because it was snowing, a rare thing, and we wanted to see it. I'd signed up at SRJC in the spring semester, and had probably moved to Santa Rosa in the late spring or early summer. At the end of the semester, though, I hadn't enough to take my mind off myself. There were occasional anxiety attacks on campus, where I'd spend hours in the cafeteria or in pleasant weather outside, keyed up on coffee and cigarettes and the pure excitement of so many new people and ideas, and fixating on sounds and colors and light; I remember chanting over and over, internally I hope but perhaps even aloud,

> *brown and yellow*
> *braun und gelb*
> *brun et jaune*
> *brown and yellow...*

And then, when classes ended, and fellow-students went their various ways, and there was no way I could really go home again to my own family, I fell into a depression, consoling myself with coffee and pie in the daytime, brandy and hot water at night. And one morning I hauled myself out of bed and pulled on a pair of trousers and lit a cigarette, and as soon as I flicked the cigarette lighter I noticed a sphere of blue flame surrounding my right hand, curious, I thought, I've never seen anything like that before, and then there was a loud noise and I was outside, my cabin was afire, the skin of my left arm hung down from my fingertips like a gauntlet turned inside-out, and policemen and firemen were looking at me anxiously.

They bundled me into the back seat of a police car and started up the engine. Where are we going, I asked. To the county hospital, one of the cops replied. It's too far, I said, there's a hospital right up this street, take me there. And they did; and the next thing I recall is lying on a gurney looking up at a doctor and a couple of nurses, and hearing the doctors say there was no point in doing much, he isn't going to make it. I was angry and showed it, I think; and I think I remember a nurse looking at me startled but perhaps with some encouragement. And then it was three days later, I was told; and a nurse said that it was a miracle that I had survived, and that I owed God a lifetime of gratitude — for this was a Catholic hospital.

I was soon transferred to the Sebastopol hospital where Dr. Sharrocks again peered down at me gravely, speaking calmly and reassuringly, but clearly concerned. I was all right from the waist down, but very badly burned above. Most of his skin grafts were gone from my left arm; one nipple was completely gone; all my acne scars were gone.

The fire had caused quite a stir, I'm sure: someone showed me the newspaper coverage of it early on. My little cabin was completely demolished, and with it all my books and papers: the only thing that survived was my suede jacket, and it was badly damaged. I gave a certain amount of thought to my situation, to the cause of this predicament, to how I should respond to the people around me.

Friends came to visit, and my parents and my brothers: they must have been aghast at what they saw, but they made a brave show. I played a little chess with my brother Jim. My violinist friend Charles came up all the way from Los Angeles to sit and talk; he told me about a new kind of music, in which one pitch of the octave, once sounded, couldn't be heard again until all the other eleven were played, always in the same order; and a few days later, after he'd gone back, and after I'd recovered the use of my right hand and arm, I wrote a few pieces for violin and piano using the system.

One day Mom brought me an envelope that had arrived at home, addressed to me in a familiar hand but lacking a return address. She opened it and handed me a terse note, undated and unsigned:

baby born Sept. 6 1954

It was the first and last communication I'd had with my wife, who I hadn't realized was expecting a baby. It seemed utterly unreal, asked for no response, came from nowhere, was going nowhere. Mom didn't say anything about it that I can remember; I don't know if any of us ever discussed the situation.

When I was finally discharged from Palm Drive Hospital I was lodged for a month or two with a Mexican family Dad had somehow met and befriended. I don't know what the reason was for this: I'd probably exhausted the patience of my grandparents, who might not have wanted to expose my younger cousins to me; and I was undoubtedly too notorious to be taken in again by the nice elderly couple I'd stayed with for a few weeks in Santa Rosa, related somehow to my grandparents. It was all the same to me; I drifted into and out of a fog. I watched television and talked to my Mexican landlady, a nice, simple woman who spoke no English and read no Spanish; I think I was supposed to be teaching her a little English, but we didn't have that much to talk about.

Gradually I recovered through the fall and winter of 1954. I had to do exercises to bring my hands back, and for a while I sat in on pottery classes in a Sebastopol studio, where I clumsily made a tall skinny black vase that we still have, and a whimsical platter with a fish carved into it in relief — I think I'd seen by then the film in which Picasso gets up from his lunch, taking the skeleton of a sole he'd just eaten, and presses it into a greenware dinner-plate waiting for him in his studio.

By the spring semester I was well enough to go back to classes. I think it was then that I took a semester of jewelry shop, again to steady my hands and increase their strength. Arlyn and Dick continued to provide some sympathy and friendship, and Jack McLean helped, and so did another older woman, a very sympathetic Dutch woman, Mary van der Hoeven, a potter who was in my jewelry class. And I collaborated on the literary club publication, *First Leaves*, helping select some of the contents. Gradually the burns healed. So did the emotional upheaval. For the time being, because of the damage to my hands, musical instruments were out of the question. I took one class in theory, but couldn't concentrate on it. The instructor, though, freshly arrived on campus, did what he could to keep me interested. He was a good violinist, and I showed him the pieces I'd written in the hospital — *Eight Banalities* I'd called them, in a far-fetched pun on "atonalities," and with the precedent of Francis Poulenc's *Banalités* in mind, though my music was influenced more by the shallow ironies of Larry Elgart's *Music for Barefoot Ballerinas*.

Mr. Ogle liked them enough to make a tape-recording, with Joseph Halprin accompanying. I wasn't privy to the rehearsals or the recording; in fact I think it was all arranged as a surprise for me, a get-well gift. And it did raise my morale a bit: for the second time I was able to hear something I'd composed — "Rain Has Fallen" having been the first — and it seemed both natural and unexpected, as if the music had been there before I'd written it down, though clearly, in spite of its awkward reminiscences of Ravel and Shostakovitch and Larry Elgart, I was the only one who had heard it until then.

Santa Rosa Junior College, 1955

6: Berkeley Between Marriages, 1955-1957

IN THE SUMMER, ALMOST completely recovered, I found myself back in Berkeley. Gramp fitted out the basement room for me, and I tried hard to fit into his household again. It had changed in the five or six years since I was last a member of the family. Gram was confined to her wheelchair, spending virtually all her time at home, only occasionally being lifted into the Hudson for a drive to the doctor or to church. Aunt Barbara was teaching school, and spent her spare time sequestered in her own bedroom, smoking and drinking Coca-Cola. Gramp was retired; he was in his early seventies; but he continued to work odd jobs as a painter and paper-hanger, and when I'd sufficiently recovered I helped him with some of those jobs — clumsily and without any will. How patient he was with me!

I came upstairs for meals, quiet ones in the family room, where Craig refused any vegetables except frozen peas, and where we had delicious chicken fricassee, and hand-cut noodles, and dinner rolls, for Gramp had made sure the counters were low enough for Gram to do her beloved baking and jam-making from her wheelchair. Most of the time I stayed downstairs in my bedroom, where I read or listened to records.

The others tried to indulge me, tried to bring me out of myself. I remember Aunt Barbara saying they'd enjoyed hearing the Grieg concerto once when I'd been playing a recording of it down in my bedroom, but I assumed this was really a veiled complaint at the volume setting on my phonograph. (When she and Gramp were at work I tried to play its opening measures on Gram's old upright piano, where I also tried to master the Schubert German Dances I'd been assigned back at Chapman; but I lost interest quickly.) And once, I remember, everyone gathered in the family room to listen as I managed to get KSRO on the AM radio: Mr. Ogle had recorded my *Banalities*, Joe Halpin capably playing the piano accompaniment, and it was somehow being broadcast on some student program. But none of us, not my grandparents, or Aunt Barbara, or even I, knew what should happen next after this inexplicable turn of events.

Gramp apparently tried to find out. A neighbor, Charles Cushing, was a professor of music at the University, and one day I found myself talking to him in his living-room; there were a great many books, and rugs; Dr. Cushing smoked a bent-stem pipe, and had a Van Dyke beard; and he asked me to sit with him at the piano and sight-read some duets, the Stravinsky *Pièces faciles*, I think. Years later his widow gave me a letter he'd sent to someone at the San Francisco Conservatory, referring to me as badly raised, "in a cabbage-patch" in fact, but perhaps worth some attention.

But I was not sent to the Conservatory, probably because of the expense. Instead I was enrolled somehow at San Francisco State College, on the far edge of San Francisco; and there in addition to one music class — what, I no longer recall — I determined to study English literature.

Mr. Meller had inspired me. He'd made me realize by then that teaching was my most probable career, and teaching music seemed to me a much less enjoyable prospect than teaching English. I suppose he'd become a "role model," even though he'd asked, soon after we'd met, why I'd set aside a "language" I knew — music — rather than continue with it. To teach as he did, in a quiet, intellectually comfortable place like Santa Rosa Junior College, seemed an attractive profession. This decision no doubt pleased Gramp and Mom, and relieved Dad and Gram; and San Francisco State College had evolved from a Teachers' College, part of the network the state of California had established a century before for the instruction of future public-school teachers who presumably would not need the more expensive and somewhat grander education offered by the

University.

SF State had recently moved from a cramped quarters downtown to an expansive campus out near the beach, far from any place I'd known until then. For a time I rode to classes with another student, but before long schedules favored a more independent approach, and I took the electric train from Berkeley to downtown San Francisco, then a streetcar out to school. Toward the end of the semester this became so inefficient that I lobbied my family to pay the rent, thirty dollars a month as I recall, for a good-sized bedroom in a comfortable home on Dorantes Street, over the west portal of the long streetcar tunnel under Twin Peaks. This was a short ride from school, and gave me, for the first time in my life, a normal, quiet, comfortable room of my own.

The house was owned by a quiet, discreet couple, elderly in my view, whose own children had long since moved away to establish their own quiet, discreet households. I'm sure they looked on me with some sympathy; perhaps my grandparents had had some discussions with them. In any case the room was kept up for me; I think I took breakfast with them; other meals were taken in the campus cafeteria.

I had by then discovered a shop in Berkeley, Contemporary Arts, that sold and rented arts and crafts items, and I rented a small abstract sculpture of a reclining nude, a piece in the Henry Moore tradition; and an expressionist painting in oils on Masonite of a standing bull, looking vaguely like a cave painting. And I began collecting books to replace the small but lamented library I'd lost in the fire in Santa Rosa.

I was writing by fits and starts, keeping a journal and trying my hand at verse. One of my classes was in modern literature, which introduced me to literary irony: I read *The Love Song of J. Alfred Prufrock* and Samuel Beckett's *Molloy* and e.e. cummings, and I tried writing fast, lyrical, punning, impressionist poems about my experiences walking the streets of San Francisco, having skimmed translations and even (though I could not understand them) the original versions of poems by Rimbaud and Verlaine. Mr. Meller had asked me to stay in touch, and I sent him one of these; he replied with the laconic observation that there might not be too long a future in a dedication to the writing of poems about poems.

I was haunting used bookstores and record stores by now. I bought the Modern Library Giant edition of *Ulysses* at the Joyce Bookshop, how appropriate, on Berkeley's Telegraph Avenue; and I bought second-hand paperback copies, when I could find them, of Beckett; and I tried my hand at binding some of these, re-sewing the signatures (for I snobbishly bought only those paperbacks that had sewn signatures) and covering them in boards, even with gold-leaf titles; kits for doing this sort of thing were sold in the bookstores. Books were still sacred objects: I'd been taught to respect them, and had learned spontaneously to covet them, no longer eating the torn-off dog-eared corners of their pages.

Special dispensation had to be negotiated for me to declare a major, but somehow I found myself a junior in college, majoring in English literature. I took a course in Symbolic Logic, which did little for me but convince me of the truth of a model "if...then" construction: if it is raining, then the streets are wet. And I took that course in modern literature, English 101, an upper-division course though I was quite unqualified, not having taken any prerequisites but one. This was taught by a serious, no-nonsense lady who bristled at my eccentricities but approved the originality of whatever analytical thinking I could prove, and I began to taste the pleasures of arguing unconventional (as it seemed then to me) views of, say, Virginia Woolf's *To the Lighthouse*, as I had the year before, in Santa Rosa, in a completely irreverent paper comparing Buddhism, Zoroastrianism, and Christianity for an admiring but mystified teacher of world history.

Another course was taught by Herbert Blau, a stage director

who had recently formed an acting company in San Francisco, The Actors' Workshop. Somehow he got wind of my musical interests — I think I had asked his advice when I wanted permission from the poet James Broughton to set a poem of his to music: this was my first completed piece since the violin pieces.

I'd found the poem in a thin broadside, *The Ballad of Mad Jenny* I think it was, in the old City Lights Bookshop in San Francisco's North Beach. By the middle 1950s paperback books were firmly a part of publishing, and City Lights mixed in as many as were available among its shelves, where I also gravitated to the cheap Modern Library edition and, out of curiosity but never for purchase because of their cost, the finer New Directions editions from James Laughlin. Upstairs, though, in a sunlit room reached by a narrow and rickety staircase, there was a gathering of broadsides and chapbooks, whose bold covers and eccentric typography delighted me. I was particularly drawn to two: Paul Blackburn's *The Dissolving Fabric* and this thin, purple-covered pamphlet of Broughton's. It didn't matter to me one way or another that Broughton was a gay man; in fact I had no idea he was; I knew nothing as yet of homosexuality.

I was drawn, too, to James Joyce's slight lyrics. I had already set "Rain has fallen," and now I set "Bright cap and streamers" for voice and soprano recorder, because I was playing recorder a bit then; it was the only wind instrument I could afford to own. For the first time I was playing with meters; the time-signature changed almost every measure, with many sevens and fives derailing the steady eighth-note rhythm. I don't know whether I played it for Blau or whether I simply showed it to him, but he was sufficiently impressed with something to suggest that I write music for a production of T.S. Eliot's *Sweeney Agonistes* that he had in mind, whether for Actors' Workshop or (more likely) a student production I do not know. We met at least once and discussed it, but I shied away from anything so public and so elaborate: I was not ready.

The bookstores, City Lights, North Beach, Berkeley's Arts and Crafts Co-Op and Telegraph Avenue: I was ranging farther afield. I visited Gram and Gramp almost weekly, taking care not to smoke on their ground, though aunt Barbara once mentioned, maliciously I thought, in the presence of the whole family, that she'd seen me downtown the other day, with a cigarette in my mouth. Gramp was, I thought, critical of the style I was evolving for myself, and saddened by my apparent rejection of any serious subject; Gram was as always indulgent and optimistic. Poor woman! She had given birth to four sons as well as her five daughters: the oldest, Charles, had died of "creeping paralysis"; Clay came back from prison camp a wreck, took to drink, and died in an automobile accident; the youngest, Bobby, could never hold a job and was functionally illiterate — only uncle David had amounted to anything: a banker, he'd worked for years after the war in Samoa, where my cousins Rick and Steven grew up; and then only recently come back to settle out near Walnut Creek, where the walnut groves and cow-pastures through which we'd driven only a few years earlier were being filled for miles around with new communities.

Perhaps in order to learn more (if only by exposure) about the musical theater, when I was thinking about *Sweeney Agonistes*, I had found an innovative theater downtown in San Francisco, Irma Kay's Opera Ring, so called because it produced musical theater in the round. She had installed a bare-bones theater in a former auto garage on South Van Ness, across the busy street from Mel's Drive In; and here I attended rehearsals of the Brecht-Weill *Threepenny Opera* in the American premiere of Eric Bentley's translation, and, later, Weill's moody *Lady in the Dark*, whose allusions to psychotherapy went right over my head in spite of my brief experience with Dr. Ross: the narrative and plot were of no interest whatsoever; it was the music, the lighting, the steady progressive rhythm of the blocking and then the staging rehearsals that fascinated me. I sat in on these rehearsals quietly, unobtrusively, never asking questions, tolerated by Miss Kay perhaps because of some conversation she'd had with Blau, and because I was willing to run across the street for pots of coffee and trays of sandwiches.

Neither music nor literature was really taking hold, in spite of my courses at State College and my infrequent correspondence with Mr Meller. I was restless and spent a fair amount of time simply getting from one place to another, on foot or by streetcar. It was a long way from San Francisco State to North Beach, let alone to Berkeley. I practiced the recorder a bit, listened to records a bit, browsed the second-hand bookshops quite a bit. There was in those days a wonderful old second-hand bookstore on Telegraph Avenue, in a block soon to be torn down for the ugly new Student Union: Creed's Books, whose street-facing room was jammed with books in tightly spaced shelves and piles on the floor, and behind that large room was a series of successively smaller and lower-ceilinged rooms, damper and damper and increasingly dim; and here I found a treasure, the out-of-print *The Beautiful and Damned* by F. Scott Fitzgerald, for I had already perfected the art of seeking titles unlikely to be found, rather than methodically reading my way through the books I could easily obtain. (Just as I had evolved a decided preference for buying books rather than borrowing them from a library, and, I'm afraid, for having a book rather than necessarily reading it.)

There was a small shelf of orchestral scores in one of Creed's back rooms, and one day as I was entering I saw a girl, her back to me, slipping a pocket score into her purse. She hesitated when she became aware of me, and instead of stealing it she wound up buying it: Bartók's *Concerto for Orchestra*. I had recently acquired a recording of it, attracted by the cover which reproduced a Braque still-life, then fascinated by the sounds, the mysterious rising fourths of the opening, the lilting five-four dance of the scherzo, and the fast nervous drive of the finale. We walked down Telegraph Avenue in the afternoon sunlight to a local restaurant — there were not yet any coffee houses or cafés in Berkeley; the Joyce Bookshop had not yet been transformed into the Piccolo Café, later the Mediterraneum.

We sat at a table in back; she bought me a cup of coffee and I picked out for her the opening of the third movement on a piano that stood nearby, and we struck up a friendship that was strictly Platonic and quite brief but meaningful to me; it was the first such friendship since Santa Rosa. She lived in a tiny cottage since torn down for a parking lot, just west of Telegraph Avenue in the middle of a block; and there we sat and smoked and drank coffee and listened to music. A favorite recording of hers was Germaine Montero's *Songs of Parisian Nights*, for this girl could read and speak French; and this inspired me to become more familiar with the poets of the texts of those songs, and with Apollinaire and Sartre; and before long I was returning to the unfinished, lyrical, mostly unaccompanied setting of a poem I'd found in my well-worn copy of *Mid-Century French Poets*, Edouard Dujardin's:

> *O dame de la profonde*
> *que faîte-vous à la surface*
> *attentive à ce-que se passe*
> *regardant la montre a mon heure...*

This girl — her name was Nadia — fascinated me and engaged me, but did not interest me romantically. I was legally free for romance; divorce papers had mysteriously been filed even before the gas explosion that had nearly done me in the year before. But I had sworn to myself never to fall in love again, and had meticulously put the oath in writing in my journal, adding, for I was beginning to grow a bit more realistic, that if I were to fall for a girl she would have to conform to an ideal, she must have a face like a Modigliani, must be spirited and intelligent, must know French and music, must be interested in me and my ideas, must listen quietly and conduct herself with reserve, but maintain absolute equality with me, sure of herself and objective, though supportive and sympathetic, with me.

Of course there was no danger of ever meeting such a paragon. Yet when one night I made the trek to Gaye's apartment in Berkeley, on Walnut Street, where she had settled with three roommates the year before, on transferring from Santa Rosa to the university in Berkeley, there was the girl I had so completely described, and I was immediately entranced. I had always felt myself to be quite unattractive, and had long since perfected a defense mechanism: I made myself even more so, dressing eccentrically, continuing to wear an eye-patch once prescribed to my little brother Tim to cure his wandering eye, and suggested to me to train a weak eye to approach the other's acuity. (The famous photograph of Joyce in his patch was perhaps a stronger influence.)

I postured with my pipe and tobacco, and clomped about in engineer's boots, and dismissed the opinions of others, and did everything I could to conform to the description of a savant that I had read, long since, in a Classics Edition Mom had given to me, even before my fire in Santa Rosa, of Erasmus's *Praise of Folly*: "Invite a wise man to a party, and he will dance like a cow; invite him to a feast and he will spoil the company, either with troublesome discourse or morose silence."

But Gaye had invited me not to a feast but to a casual dinner-party of some sort, and I had arrived with my share of the food: a loaf of French bread, unsliced but halved, and slathered with garlic butter and cheddar cheese, the whole riding in a heavy glazed terra-cotta dish, decorated with an expressionist fish. This was warmed in the oven, and the cheap red wine was poured, and we sat around conversing and playing games and listening, occasionally, to music. And I gazed at Lindsey — for she was my *bien-aimée avant la lettre*.

She had declared a "group major" at the University, in France and the French Colonies — for Algeria and Indo-China were still within the French community in those days — and she was taking music courses, marking up the score to Beethoven's Op. 59/1 string quartet for a music-appreciation course, and singing in the chorus for a performance of Beethoven's *Missa Solemnis*, to which I took an immediate and jealous dislike. She was soft-spoken but strong-willed and very, very beautiful. Her roommates were fun and interesting — Gaye, whom I'd known for a few years, was intelligent and literary; Bette was warm-blooded and fun-loving in her Italian-American way; Sharon was tall and very blonde and athletic but cool and quiet. All four were friendly and unafraid, mature it seemed to me, interested in every corner of college life — athletics, studies, entertainment, eating, drinking. And, wonder of wonders, they seemed to like me, and to listen to me, and they gradually drew me out of myself and the evasive aspects of the enthusiasms I'd dedicated myself to, and drew me to look at those enthusiasms for their intrinsically meaningful and entertaining qualities rather than primarily as fortresses into which I could hide from the difficuties and complexities of the external world.

Before long I wanted to be back in Berkeley, to be nearer Lindsey. In spite of City Lights and the Opera Ring I had never really been a San Franciscan, had not taken advantage of even such free cultural offerings as the city library or the museums. And by now I had dropped out of college at San Francisco State. I spent a month or two back in Gramp's basement, and looked around for a job and a room, and before long found both, within a single block, and not a block from the snug modern apartment the four girls had just moved to, on Le Conte Street, just across the street from the house Gramp and I had worked on only two or three years earlier. I was back in the food business, cooking, then managing in a sense a restaurant called The Northgate, in that block of Euclid Avenue that I'd often taken when playing hooky from church services; and I rented a furnished room, much like the one I'd had in San Francisco, around the corner on Ridge Road.

Up the street was a new friend, an older man named Paul Buonaccorsi, quiet and intelligent, Catholic and fond of boxing matches — his only inexplicable fault that I could see. He was a calming influence, but I spent more time with the girls on Le Roy, Bette, Sharon, and Lindsey — Gaye by then having moved elsewhere. Here we passed the time with crossword puzzles, and delighted conversations about Herb Caen's column in the San Francisco *Chronicle*, and the *Peanuts* comic strip; Lindsey and I spent hours listening to the Castelnuovo-Tedesco Guitar Concerto, and the Beethoven Second Piano Concerto, and of course the quartet Op. 59/1 that she'd studied; and to the original-cast recording of *High Society*. One memorable day we went all the way to San Francisco to see the movie, just released, of *Oklahoma!*. Other times we just drank enough beer for me to pass out quietly on the couch.

And I spent long hours in the Northgate, a single large, open room, seating perhaps sixty or eighty people if full, which it rarely was. There was no table service: customers placed their orders and waited for them to be cooked at the register. Often enough I would be the only person working, starting at breakfast time, cooking bacon and eggs and pancakes, and switching to hamburgers and grilled cheese sandwiches a few hours later. I don't recall the dinner; perhaps we closed by then; perhaps an entirely different crew took over. George V. Cooper, who ran the Northgate, taught me tricks to add to the trade I'd taken up in Los Angeles and Santa Rosa: add a quarter teaspoon of salt to the basket when making a pot of coffee; put celery salt in the egg salad; don't squeeze the grease out of the hamburger when it's cooking if it's ordered well done. I enjoyed the job and felt rewarded when George left me alone with it, and before long he was calling me the daytime manager, though there was never more than one other person working with me, and that was rare.

For one grueling week, in May of 1956, the restaurant was closed, for George was giving it a thorough cleaning and minor remodel. I worked around the clock once or twice during that week, all within the fifty dollars a week I was getting. But of course I took a number of meals there too, and my room rent was only twenty-eight dollars a month, thirty when another room became available up Ridge Road in a detached cottage, with a separate entrance and a private bath. I had enough money, in fact, to buy my first car, a beautiful maroon 1947 Mercury convertible that I'd fallen in love with when I saw it on a lot. The top was in bad shape, but the car only cost a hundred dollars, and it made me feel very sporty.

And I had enough money to buy books, and to begin to keep occasional accounts, some of which I still have. I bought Gertrude Stein's *Four in America*. I ordered, from Blackwell's Books in England, books by Woolf and Lawrence, and Dorothy Richardson's four-volume novel *Pilgrimage*, for the modern English novel course at San Francisco State had introduced me to the Stream of Consciousness, and I was enthralled. I subscribed to a discerning book club that had just been established, The Reader's Subscription, and from them I acquired *Finnegans Wake*, the collected e.e. cummings, and Virginia Woolf's *A Writer's Diary*. And I continued to visit the Arts and Crafts Coop, buying another painting, a copper mask, and an iron sculpture of an Etruscan warrior. I never gave a moment's thought to model railroads: I had joined an intellectual elite, or was trying to, and distancing myself as far as possible from childhood and adolescence, recent though they had been.

At the same time I was writing, writing. There are pages of poem titles, carefully grouped into categories: Love songs, Epiphanies; Nocturnes; Observations; Parodies; Poems à clef. All were Joyce-ridden, either with silly far-fetched puns, in the manner (but lacking the substance!) of *Finnegans Wake*, or light, self-pitying lyrics, after the manner of *Chamber Music*. And these poems were merely occasional writing: for I was working on a novel.

And I was overcome, consumed, quite possessed by my growing passion. A journal entry dated May 16, 1956 is explicit:

> I know I'm going on at it too much, but just another word. I seem to be possessed of that dreadful and dangerous capacity for analyzing and understanding completely my actions and thoughts at the moment of their manifestation, as if an objective discrete person were dwelling within me. I know I am in the process of 'falling in love', but I'm not sure I shall be more than simply in the process. I want to... I'm not sure what I want. I want a soft brushing of lips, full of transient intimacy, significant dispassion: I want something gentle and tender like the way that girl — Sharon? — so tenderly drunkenly said of her date: —Jerry was so sweet. So sweet.
>
> But I have to make money: enough for food and an apartment, a car; and still I must go to school. I know what I want. I want to get married and raise children. Is that such a folly? What else is there? I can write or something and maybe make something fine, but it's still dead. I want living things: a rose, a cat, a child. I want to be surrounded with life, and love, and warmth, and a soft enveloping pervasion of — intimate tenderness. 'So we beat on, boats against the current, drifting back ceaselessly into the past.'

The quote is from the end of *The Great Gatsby*, and misremembered: "borne back ceaselessly," not "drifting," though

God knows I was adrift. I made a concerted campaign, though, and by the end of the month found myself loved in return, and a week later, on Lindsey's twenty-first birthday, in spite of her roommates' concerned reservations about any future value I might have, she agreed to marry me.

Over the summer of 1956 I continued working on the novel and worried at sketches for music: the concerto for oboe and horn; a piano sonata; a quartet. I flirted with the idea of writing a memoir, and I'm sorry now I didn't; it would make the present job a lot easier. I wrote dozens of poems, none more than a single page long; and I read. A fascinating bookstore had been opened across the street from the Northgate by Fred Cody, who gambled on offering for sale nothing but paperbacks. For some reason he asked my advice on stock, and I urged him to include books in foreign languages: he brought in a complete Pirandello, and Moravia, and all the standard and modern French authors. Lindsey was of course reading French literature for her degree, and I had a lot of catchup facing me.

I also had to take my place within her family, and over the summer we made a number of trips to her family's farm. Lindsey and I had a similar background, though only in form, not in details. Born in Chicago, she'd lived her first ten or twelve years in a suburb in Indiana; then after the war her family had settled on a farm south of Healdsburg, in Sonoma county, ten or fifteen miles north of Blank Road. I was the oldest of four boys; Lindsey was the oldest of five girls. My childhood, when I was not with my grandparents, was not so unfamiliar with poverty: Lindsey's family, while certainly never poor, was certainly frugal. We both had grown up wearing hand-me-downs and homemade clothes, and we were both familiar with chores and with bricolage, making things do, or making things out of whatever came to hand.

But the two households were in completely different worlds. Lindsey was amazed at the squalor on Blank Road, and I was delighted with the warmth and efficiency on Eastside Road. My parents had two cows at the most, the pigs were as often loose as penned, the cars frequently broke down. Lindsey's father had a herd of two hundred cows; he kept his machinery running smoothly; the pigs were dependably housed. Best of all, Lindsey's mother was an excellent cook, and warm and funny and affectionate, though undoubtedly bewildered with her oldest daughter's choice of a boy friend.

Lindsey's father was not bewildered; he was clearly worried. I had a terrible employment record; I was divorced; I looked weird (though I'd shaved off my first mustache, a terribly inadequate one Aunt Barbara had found laughable, when we first went up to the country to meet him); I was cocky and useless. I think he was touched, though, when I finally summoned up the nerve to ask his permission to marry Lindsey — I felt this was a necessary step, perhaps as a kind of validation of my potential. I wanted this marriage to be as different as possible from the previous, which had begun with only grudging permission from the adults involved.

Bob fascinated me. He was quiet, orderly, methodical. He ran a complex operation: the farm comprised hundreds of acres, in pasture, hay, and prunes. Bob had bought the place, with his sister and two or three brothers, when he moved out from Chicago in 1947. He was the youngest child, I think, of his Italian immigrant parents, born in a small town in the mountains west of Torino, where he lived until he was ten years old, some of the time with his parents, some of the time with an aunt. That had been the family pattern: his father was a *contadino*; his mother a wetnurse, who worked in Paris, coming home every two or three years to have another child of her own, who would then be cared for by an aunt so that she could go back to earning money abroad. (In those days, the last years of the Nineteenth Century, milk from mountain women was thought superior.)

The idea of a family farm did not outlast the first bad harvest, and it had to be sold; but Bob stayed on as ranch manager. He was a good and conscientious one. He hired and managed the crews, favoring loyal Mexican *braceros* whose condition and temperament must have been similar to that of the *contadini* among whom he'd grown up. He was frugal, finding the tools he needed second hand, and making them himself when necessary. He was inventive: he spent a number of hours designing a mechanical prune harvester.

He'd been an electrical engineer at the South Chicago steel works, and he was handy with all things mechanical and electrical. More than once he worked with me adjusting and tuning the engine on my Mercury, explaining what was wrong with the flywheel when I had to rock the car, in gear, in order to free the starter-motor to do its work. He had designed and built the big concrete-block milk barn, whose gambrel roof is still, fifty years later, a landmark on Eastside Road; and he'd designed a marvelous system of hosing down the cows' loafing area, pumping the waste out over the prune orchard as manure — a lovely application of recycling whose ironic symbolism was not lost on me.

We all called the place The Ranch, and this must be why I have never been able to join my brothers in so describing our miserable family compound on Blank Road. Not so slowly, and with no difficulty, Lindsey's home and family were becoming my own, and I neglected my own parents and brothers, and forgot or suppressed my own upbringing. On an early visit to The Ranch I fell ill with a high fever, and was in bed for a number of days, weak and confused: at the time we thought it was the flu, or perhaps mononucleosis, but years later when new tests had evolved I turned out to have had a form of hepatitis at one time, and this may have been that occasion. In any case Agnes, Lindsey's mother, looked after me as solicitously as if I were her own son.

Things were not idyllic in this household. Bob and Agnes

had a strained relationship when I first met them, and it declined further over the next few years, until ultimately they did not speak to one another, communicating on the rare occasions it was necessary through their children — including me, when I was visiting. The younger girls, of course, were of little interest to me; I knew nothing about girls or their interests, though the youngest one did have some promise, since she took up the clarinet, and enjoyed art projects in school. I spent my hours at The Ranch reading, or watching Bob work in the shops, or writing: for my novel was moving along, and I brought my stylish portable typewriter with me, a streamlined Olympia which I favored for its European accents and its variable spacing. Poor Lindsey did most of the typing, sitting at the maple dropleaf table in the sunny knotty-pine-panelled dining room.

I had planned to resume classes at San Francisco State College in the fall of 1956. I had passed my landmark twenty-first birthday, and it was time for me to get my degree and get to work. But I soon dropped out of school. I told myself, in my Satyrday Review, that it was "impossible to think, either scholastically or originally, in the college atmosphere, and that I couldn't spare two more years not thinking." I was intent on finishing my novel, but creative thought was only a part of my quandary: I must also have been contemplating the balance of that kind of creative life — the writer's life — with the responsibilities that marriage would involve, the responsibilities I'd promised Bob I would assume.

Clearly I'd learned something since my first attempt at marriage, when marriage meant the establishing of a domestic life of my own, carrying out my own garbage, hanging my own laundry. (The enormity of providing for that garbage and that laundry hadn't occurred to me.) Now, four years later, I longed for more than a household; I wanted life itself. But what would happen to my cherished individuality, and to my role of artist? It was, by then, the only vocation I could imagine for myself.

One model, I suppose, was Mr. Meller, who'd published two fine novels of place and family, *Home is Here* and *Roots in the Sky*, and then settled into a quiet and as far as I could see rewarding life teaching at a two-year college in a comfortable small town. The other models were F. Scott Fitzgerald and, of course, James Joyce; but the domestic situations they had evolved for themselves, while fascinating and romantic, didn't seem too stable or comfortable — and were, though I didn't give this a lot of thought at the time, terribly unfair to the women involved.

Most of this interior discussion went on subconsciously. Between July 1956 and March 1957 I made only one journal entry, over two days in October, when I came to the realization quoted above. But if I didn't think the situation through logically, let alone publicly, I can infer from journal entries about my music that in an interior fashion I realized analysis and care should be brought to this momentous decision — my own analysis and care of course: I had no interest in looking for any outside help, professional or otherwise. So I had abandoned those early plans for an ambitious series of compositions: "they would lead to artistic failure. Why? Inadequate planning. Take the oboe-horn concerto: pure fumbling rhapsody. Cure: outlining, logical form..." (Journal entry, July 14 1956).

Again, two weeks later: "...to realize that I have at last achieved the stability of loving with comfort and ease, this helps me a great deal. I need no longer fear myself — so I need no longer fear. But fear has become something of a habit with me — to break it means constant watching, and checking whenever it appears."

By now I was working for the railroad; I don't remember why or how. At first it was night work, in the freight yards near the big oil refinery in Richmond, not far from where Dad used to take me to Block Warden meetings in the old brick firehouse. Here I spent hours sitting next to the small coal-burning stove, now and then going out into the black night with a strong flashlight to record the numbers of freight cars as they were shunted onto this siding or that. It was pleasant enough work, though I hated the smell of the air, heavy with fumes; and I related badly to the other workers, who were mistrustful of my abilities and, for all I know, of my very stability.

After a few weeks of this I was transferred to a day job supervising the loading of boxcars at the Sugar Dock. This was near the old shipyards. Every day a boat came in loaded with pallets of sugar from the C&H refinery in Crockett. These were unloaded by a very skilful driver of a fork-lift truck, a machine entirely new to me. The pallets were set down near the freight cars, sometimes even within them, and the sugar was stacked by gangs of black stevedores. There were four or five sidings, each with six or eight boxcars; each siding had its supervisor (white, of course, in those days) and crew.

Stacking those carloads was a complex operation, because the sugar was in packages of various shapes and sizes — bags and boxes, ranging from two pounds to one hundred, individually or in units; brown, white, or raw. And nearly all these cars were being sent LCL, "less than carload": some of the boxcar would be unloaded at a first destination, and the rest would go on to another, perhaps to four or five destinations in all; and the contents had to be level, from one end of the boxcar to the other, after each partial unloading, lest they shift and tear in the rough-and-tumble of switching and shunting that is the norm in rail freight operations.

On the first day I was given the simplest of carloads: only one kind of package, only one destination. It was simply a matter of figuring out how high to stack the first bags, so that at the end of the operation the car would be evenly filled. Even this eluded me, but I was immediately taught how to proceed: one of the stevedores said to show the crew the "manifest," or description of the car's contents, and then step aside and let them do their work — which, after all, they'd been doing for years.

This taught me a lot, though little of it was apparent at the time. Flow control is best left to itself. The real work is done by the workers. Systems have evolved for maximum employment. Laziness, physical effort, intellectual acuity — all are fungible. And I was working daylight hours; the climate at the dock was pleasant and the air reasonably clean (if you stayed out of the boxcars). I watched the loads being stacked, cheerful and patient, and daydreamed; and I spent the long lunch hours sitting in the sun in my convertible, continuing my reading of *Ulysses*, while the stevedores shot craps and joked. One of them, a very nice fellow, did some work on my car once, and when I asked what I owed him he gave me an important lesson: "You peckers think everything is about money. Give me a dictionary for my church, that's all I want." And I did give him one, an old one Mom had given me years earlier; and when one day I blew the head-gasket in my Mercury one time too many I gave him that as well, for fifty dollars in return; and Bob gave me a little Nash Rambler he'd had for a few years, and was no longer using.

In the meantime I'd been transferred once again: I suppose my utter inadequacy at planning complex carloads had been revealed. The new job was in San Francisco, night work again, and again as a yard clerk, recording the numbers of freight cars. This was harder, though, for in addition to stationary cars that had been dropped off at one siding or another I was expected to record long lists of cars as they actually went by. This involved standing close to the tracks in the dark, cradling a lantern in the crook of my left arm, writing the numbers down on slips of paper on a clipboard, picking out the numbers as they slipped past, faster and faster, until soon enough I was seeing a number go by while trying to remember the one that had gone before — and actually writing the one I'd seen before that.

Fortunately this happened only two or three times a shift, and otherwise I'd be assigned to walk out to various sidings and check on the cars that had already been shunted there. This took me to dark sleeping factories and warehouses in what seemed to me a mysterious and romantic part of town, one I'd never before seen, dark and electric; and the scents of sweat, oil, the salt air off the Bay, and the sounds of unseen labor and machinery, were both exhilarating and in a curious way hypnotic; this nocturnal life was an entirely different one from the daytime one of reading and writing, cruising the bookstores, and conversing with my friends on LeRoy Street.

And the work seemed steady, and the pay not bad; so by the beginning of the next year, 1957, after a wonderful Christmas, as it seemed to me, with Lindsey's family, we began to think of when and how and where to get married. Lindsey would graduate from the University in June, when she turned twenty-two, and could turn her full attention to her own life, and to mine.

By then I had virtually lost touch with my parents' marriage, which was even shakier than Lindsey's parents'. Mom had learned to drive, had finished college at a Santa Rosa campus of San Francisco State, and had got a job teaching in a grammar school in a remote corner of Sonoma county, near Fort Ross. She lived for a few months in a rented room on a sheep ranch, then was given her own cabin. John and Tim, the two youngest boys, joined her there, but Jim, who was in high school, stayed on Blank Road with Dad. Later for some reason Mom moved to a rented cabin near Jenner, where one day Lindsey and I visited. Dad was there, and Mom was in tears; she told me she needed help, and asked me to tell Dr. Ross of her situation.

I didn't really know what the situation was, and had only her version of it. Still Lindsey and I drove as fast as we could along the narrow, winding river road, then to Dr. Ross's office. I turned things over in my mind on the frantic drive through Pocket Canyon: Mom had been in touch with Dr. Ross more than I'd known, and not only about me. But when I told him what was happening he seemed not terribly concerned, as if it were all a familiar story, and I was reassured. The history of my parents' marriage is complicated and probably very interesting, but I don't really know it. The last time I remember seeing them together in any public setting, where they were maintaining the semblance of a normal relationship, was on May 11, 1957, when Lindsey and I were married.

with Lindsey and her sister Sandra, at Lindsey's graduation,
UC Berkeley, June 1957

7: Starting a Family, 1957-1963

WE'D CHOSEN A BERKELEY CHURCH at Walnut and Cedar, just up the street from Las Casitas, the stucco apartment where I'd first met Lindsey a year earlier. Lindsey's parents and mine were present, all of them no doubt full of misgivings and skeptical of the institution of marriage. The setting was incongruous: neither Lindsey nor I was attending any kind of church, or felt ourselves religious in any usual sense; Mom and Dad had never attended church or even spoken any opinion on the matter; Bob and Agnes were from Catholic families but had not attended Mass since childhood. But I wanted a church marriage: I think I felt it necessary to have this marriage not so much blessed as confirmed by every social institution.

Perhaps I was subconsciously recalling that definition: "the serious and social attitude toward that which controls one's destiny." Marriage, and specifically marriage with Lindsey, was my fate, my destiny. I had in fact wanted to marry in a Catholic church, and had even investigated converting — influenced no doubt by the Joyce biography, but also by my friendship with Paul Buonaccorsi, and perhaps a romantic view of the apostasy of Lindsey's parents, who were renegade Catholics. But the priest who interviewed me sadly concluded that since I had been baptized, and since I had been married in a Christian ceremony, this subsequent marriage would be prohibited. So ended my last approach to Christianity.

Afterward we went somewhere for lunch, I think, and then to our new home, a studio apartment we'd found on the south side of campus, on Durant Avenue, across from the manorial

Women's City Club in whose basement pool, one magical day ten years earlier, I'd been taken swimming by Wiley Keys and his mother, who was no doubt a member.

We, of course, were nothing so grand. We could barely afford the rent. We slept on a sofa-bed, for the apartment was furnished with one, and ate frugally — I remember picking plums that summer from the ornamental street trees to make fruit soup with raisins, sugar and lemon peel, with a little tapioca for thickening — a recipe I'd learned a year or two earlier from Carma. We cut back on luxuries like the coffee house: we'd bought a copper Italian turnover pot, and I bought coffee beans at the Safeway, roasted them a second time on a baking sheet in the oven, and returned with them to the Safeway to grind them.

The apartment was nicely close to Telegraph Avenue and its bookstores, but it was dim and cheerless, in spite of the cheap magazine-illustration art reproductions that we glued to the walls in a desperate attempt to contrive some kind of atmosphere. But soon we found a better apartment in our price range, and we were back on the north side of town at 1313 Grove Street, an address that should have aroused my superstition but somehow did not.

We were in a fairly new stucco building, built something like a motel, with five or six apartments giving on to a porch running along its north side, up a half-flight of steps from the front garden. There was a parking lot in the rear for our Mercury and, later, our little Nash Rambler, and a real bedroom as well as a living room and an adequate kitchen. The site was perfect: Live Oak Park, where I'd played so often as a child, was a block in one direction; Garfield Junior High, where I'd gone to school, was three or four blocks in the other. The Co-op supermarket that we favored was within easy walking distance on Shattuck Avenue, and the electric F train to San Francisco; and Gramp and Gram, should I want them, were only a few blocks beyond that.

But the apartment was unfurnished. Bob and Agnes gave us the considerable gift of a beautiful brass double bed, an antique that had been given them by friends of theirs, and I made our living-room furniture — not out of automobile seats, but by setting a narrow strip of plywood on four rectangular five-gallon cans salvaged somewhere, and covering it with foam rubber and an upholstery-cloth sample bought from Bob Harris, a local hero in the student community for his inexpensive solutions to student furnishing problems.

We had bought a cheap "basket chair" made of woven straw and set on four thin rubber-tipped iron legs. At a sidewalk sale I'd bought an amateur abstract painted on a rectangular sheet of plywood: I cut off the corners, making legs of them for the artistically irregular octagon that was left over to be used as a top, and this was our coffee table. I made a good-sized speaker cabinet out of a cardboard box and mounted a scrap car-radio speaker in it, and added later to it a smaller wooden cabinet with another, smaller speaker, to which I carefully glued a half eggshell in the center, to disperse the higher frequencies; and I made a hanging lamp out of speckled fiberglass from Bob Harris, and a shoji-like screen to cover the one window that let north light into the apartment.

Here we entertained our guests. We had long evenings with a Santa Rosa friend of Lindsey's, Ed Squibb, who was very conservative politically and socially — he moved out of his apartment on learning his landlord rented to unmarried couples! — but who had an interesting mind and a bent for science and mathematics and a curiosity abouut the humanities that I was glad to satisfy.

We spent hours, too, with Carma and Jerry, the pistol-wielding boy friend she had since married, talking about life and literature. My brother Jim came to visit from time to time: Mom must have moved by then to Berkeley, to the house Gramp had helped her buy down on Rose Street, the other side of Garfield School; but I don't remember visiting her there

more than once or twice, or her coming to see us — "I don't in-
terfere," she was fond of saying when the subject was raised;
she clearly preferred this time to leave me to my own household.

Best of all, I was writing music. Arlyn, who was by now living in Berkeley to attend the university, had shown me a notice
in the student newspaper, early in the fall semester of 1957: the
drama department was looking for someone to compose inci-
dental music for a student production that winter. I answered
the call, meeting with the play's director, Robert Goldsby, and
something in our interview convinced him to give me a try. I
had no history of public performances, and had completed
really only a few pieces of music. I did have a tape recording of
the *Eight Banalities*, and I suppose I lent it to him — I never
listened to it myself, a tape-recorder being well beyond our
finances.

In any case I soon found myself cobbling together a series of
musical vignettes for this production of Tennessee Williams's
early, experimental play *Camino Real*, an odd, vaguely Symbol-
ist thing whose meaning eluded me entirely but whose magical
mood lent itself to my imagination. I was to provide the orchestra as well as the music, so I kept the forces small: trumpet, violin, flute, bassoon, piano and drums. In Santa Rosa I had already improvised a moody, jazz-like blues in five-four time,
heavily influenced by Carma's beloved *Music for Barefoot Ballerinas*, and it was easy to adapt that to this new purpose. I wrote
out a short instrumental introduction to the play, and peppered
the action with a number of shrill parodies of the *Dies irae*, for
Death was a prominent member of the cast.

It was fascinating to attend the early rehearsals, the readings
and the blocking. I'd met, somehow, a pianist, Duncan Pierce,
who was willing to play reductions of my score at the rehearsals; and through him I found a trumpeter, Phil Lesh, already a
member of the musician's union and therefore required to participate in this unpaid work under a pseudonym (he would

later trade trumpet for bass guitar and help found The Grateful Dead). I don't remember where the bassoonist came from. Duncan took on the percussion part as well, and even provided his own bongos.

Someone had told me that the flutist in the Oakland Symphony, Jean Zeiger, was willing to play new music for nothing, and I called on her, encouraged by the fact that she lived on North Street, across the street from the one childhood home I remembered fondly. But her schedule didn't permit her to help, and she recommended a student, Kendall Allphin, who lived in a shabby apartment in a Victorian cottage down on University Avenue, next to the big lot, now empty, that had been a coal-and-feed store before the War, where Dad had sewn up burlap sacks for a living when I was born.

This recommendation was the most lasting and wonderful event associated with my first appearance as a composer, for Kendall became our closest friend. I spent hours at his apartment, with Lindsey and without her, and he spent hours at ours, almost always with a jug of cheap red wine that we bought in those days for seventy-five cents a gallon, supply your own jug. He was funny and smart, musical and well-read. He was a New Englander with a broad New England accent, and had flunked out of MIT and gone to the arty Reed College in Oregon, and had as many anecdotes to tell about his early college days as I did not have about mine.

He played passable flute, but could not play the piccolo, so he resorted to a sopranino recorder for those *Dies irae* cues. He was supporting himself, after a fashion, by giving recorder lessons, mostly to elderly wives of University faculty — a tiny but regular income that would later be passed on to me.

At about this same time, in mid-December 1957, our first child was born, a girl we agreed to name Thérèse Hélène, spelled in the French way in honor of Lindsey's enthusiasms, and named for St. Teresa of Avila, the heroine of *Four Saints in Three Acts*. She was born quickly and fairly easily: Lindsey woke me in the morning and we rushed to Alta Bates Hospital, south of campus. Lindsey's parents came as soon as they were summoned, and early in the morning of December 19, a week short of Christmas and a month sooner than we might have wished, I was a father in more than fact, for this baby was right there before my fascinated eyes, and would delight and complicate my life for years to come.

Not that I was ready to accept paternal responsibility. For one reason or another I was no longer working on the railroad: instead I was doing occasional odd jobs, painting or gardening. Our kitchen cabinets were still quite empty. We lived for weeks on a huge box of canned smoked oysters given to us by Arlyn's mother, who was being romanced by a salesman of such items. Another time I made a carefully researched guess at the weight of a block of Cheddar cheese for a contest in connection with the opening of a new supermarket, and came within a few ounces of the correct answer: the prize, five pounds of Cheddar, kept us from starving for another few weeks. And soon the plums were again ripe on the street trees.

But it became clear that I had to find a real job, and a meeting with Jack McLean, who I hadn't seen in months but who remained loyally in touch from time to time, led me to the next step in my gradual acceptance of the working life. He was still sorting mail on his railroad car, a week or so on the road, then a few days off; and he convinced me of the suitability of such a schedule to an artistic life, even one complicated by marriage and fatherhood. And, he suggested, I could even attend classes at San Francisco State; where some kind of dispensation was apparently made for working students.

Lindsey spent hours with flash cards helping me memorize mail-distribution schemes so that I could qualify as a trainee for the Postal Transport Service, and I passed the test easily, placing near the top of the waiting list. But I was posted, as you might say, not to a railroad car, which was what I wanted, but to a sorting facility at the San Francisco Airport. I would have to report to work soon, in the summer of 1958; and there was no question of commuting there from Berkeley. We would have to give up our apartment and our friends and find a place in an unfamiliar setting.

It wasn't hard to find a house. We rented a real one, not an apartment; a detached three-bedroom ranch-style house with a lawn and a back yard and a two-car attached garage, on a quiet street in the beach suburb then called Pacific Manor, later incorporated with a couple of neighboring towns into the city of Pacifica. Lindsey's sister, Pat, was attending San Francisco State, and she moved in with us, helping with the rent. (I'd seen Pat, eighteen months younger than Lindsey, but had not known her, at JC, where she was taking French classes.) The basket chair was put in a corner of what seemed a vast living room, and I built a little bookcase, and the fish dish, the shiny black vase, and the expressionist painting of the bull and the hanging fiberglass lamp made, we thought, a stylish and modern furnishing; and bit by bit we managed to add other items. The baby had her own room, and I used to stand by the crib and marvel at this pretty little thing so placid in her sleep, so annoyingly imperious in her wakefulness, for Thérèse was given to tantrums; we were even prescribed a narcotic of some kind to try to calm her.

Lindsey befriended a neighbor who lived across the street, a woman of Greek heritage, who had a small child and a wonderful recipe for cookies, and the two of them pushed their strollers along the sidewalks on the rare sunny days, for Pacific Manor was in a fog belt, and weeks went by without a glimpse of the sun. There was a shopping center a few blocks away, and there we found a delicatessen that specialized for some reason in Scandinavian items, lingonberries and the like; and there was a record store where I bought LPs by Eddie Heywood and Errol Garner, for Lindsey liked piano jazz: and who does not?.

The airport was on the other side of the peninsula. I drove up the steep Manor Drive, across the ridge, and then down through San Mateo to the airport, where I worked five days a week alongside a number of other men. The mail arrived in bundles or as parcels in big canvas wheeled bins, and we tossed it into the proper bags, heavy canvas ones that went out in trucks, thin orange Nylon ones that were dispatched to airplanes. I didn't like the regularity of the hours or the commitment it required, but I had no choice. I had been involved in a minor traffic accident that spring in Berkeley, driving home from an odd job painting, and since I was uninsured I had had to post a bond in order to retain my driver's license, which of course was indispensable given our new situation. The repairs to the car were added to the expenses of the household, and while our parents helped us discreetly we did not want to impose on them — nor would they have sacrificed responsibilities to our younger siblings to bail us out. We were on our own, though never abandoned.

So I kept this job; it was the first time I kept a job through the difficulties and embarrassments and indignities that seemed to me to be the inevitable lot of the man who must work for his living. And in fact it wasn't a bad job. I enjoyed my own competence, and I enjoyed tossing the mail, like so many basketballs, into this mouth or that among the dozens that yawned open among the racks of canvas bags. I enjoyed being at the airport and seeing the airplanes come and go; I even enjoyed the smell of kerosene, which recalled work on the railroad, and even those nights without electricity when I was ten and eleven years old, only ten years before.

I had one friend, a small man as young as I, and we even entertained one another socially a few times — once driving, at his suggestion, up into the Napa valley to visit wineries: we went to Schramsberg, where I was transported by the European elegance of the grand old hawk-nosed woman who presided over the business, and by the amazing caves that had been hollowed out of the limestone by Chinese coolies a century before, and not least by the golden-yellow "hock" that came in stylish long-necked bottles covered with metallic netting. But I maintained a proud detachment from the other mail handlers, most of whom seemed uncouth. (As if I were not!) And to increase my detachment I took care to present an eccentric appearance, growing a Roman-style haircut with bangs falling over my forehead, and wearing my eternal engineer's boots, and smoking my corncob pipe.

Lindsey spent time with the Greek-American woman who lived across the street, but I had little time for socializing, since I was again taking classes at San Francisco State as well as working full-time. There were odd hours left over: I had time to assemble a Heathkit FM tuner that Lindsey had given me for Christmas — important, for Lindsey needed the intellectual stimulation provided by KPFA's public-affairs programming to offset the isolation of this sleepy seaside suburb, and I was fascinated by the occasional broadcasts of contemporary music. Kendall had introduced me to these kits, which made hi-fi more affordable. From plans in a magazine I built a real loudspeaker cabinet to replace the cardboard one, and an equalizer array to improve the playback of the many types of recording then competing among the many producers of long-playing records.

I puttered, too, with the car, the small Nash Rambler Lindsey's father had given us to replace the beloved Mercury. After the minor accident the Nash never really worked properly: I often had to manipulate its gearbox linkage manually when it was stuck in gear, and there was something wrong with the electrical system: when turning off the engine you had to turn off the ignition, whereupon the engine would keep running; then turn the headlights on, then turn them off again, whereupon the engine would stop. I never did figure out the the proper solution of that problem, but banging on the cover of the voltage regulator seemed to help.

Our first family photographs are from that year, 1958, in Sharp Park. They show Thérèse with her curly white hair in a pony-tail, sitting in the basket chair under the fiberglass hanging cylindrical lamp, next to the artfully arranged bookcase; or out on the lawn on one of the rare sunny days. Lindsey began her gardening enthusiasm here, too; we used to go to a nearby nursery with our first credit card, spending four or five dollars at a time on plants for the border.

All the time I was waiting for my name to come up on a transfer request to a railroad car or to the Berkeley post office, and before a year was out it finally came through: I was posted to the basement of the main post office in Berkeley, and by the late summer of 1958 it was time for another move. I'd had the flu or something when it was time to make the actual move from Sharp Park, and Lindsey's father appeared with a truck and a hired hand and loaded up our few possessions for the move across the Bay. What a patient and generous man!

Berkeley: Channing Way

I don't recall how we found that next home: probably from a newspaper ad. We were back on the south side again, though only technically; and in fact not that far from 1817 Bancroft, in a part of Berkeley I've always liked. We rented the uptown, east half of a onestorey brownshingle duplex whose owner, a quiet single woman in her forties who worked for a map publisher, lived on the other side. The duplex was small but very homey, set back twelve or fifteen feet from the sidewalk, behind a scrappy lawn no one really gave much thought to. There was a flight of three or four steps up to a real front porch, the kind you put a couple of chairs on, and the front door opened directly onto a large living room dominated by a massive clinker-brick fireplace at the center of the long wall opposite the door, and well lit at the south by windows looking out over the lawn. The room had a summer-cabin feel, perhaps because of that fireplace. Off that room was a tiny bathroom, just big enough for tub, sink, and toilet. There were two bedrooms, but one was really little more than a walk-in closet: this would be Thérèse's nursery.

The kitchen was hardly adequate — a Pullman-style galley, refrigerator sink and stove in a line on one windowless wall, cabinets above, no room on the parallel wall for any but the shallowest shelf. And that was it. Behind, though, there was a fine back yard, with an enormous pine tree shading the north end, and a red-fleshed "Indian" peach, and a lawn that did get some attention now and then.

And in this yard was a small shed, probably originally a toolshed of some kind. After a few months I dragged it over to the house and set it up on concrete pierblocks, tearing off one end wall and nailing it to the back wall by the kitchen door, and thus we had a breakfast room big enough for table and chairs and even a washing machine — though I always had to sit on the machine during the spin cycle, for the shed rocked alarmingly on its pierblocks.

And soon it was 1959; Lindsey and I were twenty-four years old; we lived in a fascinating place, and I had a decent job. And we had friends. One of them was a small shy fellow named Gary Jurberg, who worked at the Post Office and who had a fondness for Mahler; it was he who got me interested in what at the time was still quite unfamiliar musical territory. (A book I still have, a Penguin paperback guide called *The Symphony*, still then referred to Mahler as an amateur, and his Eighth Symphony in particular as mythic and unplayable.) At one point Gary gave me a large number of LPs, and my collection began to grow as I continued to search the used-record stores. And I began to search out the few recordings then available of music by Charles Ives: *Central Park in the Dark*; *Three Places in New England*. And one day I found what turned out to be a treasure, a ten-inch long-playing record with Janácek's wind sextet *Mladi*, and a charming little woodwind suite by a completely unknown composer, Frantisek Bartos.

I was also beginning to collect pocket editions of orchestral scores, finding them second-hand when I was lucky. I studied these fairly carefully, listening to recordings with the score when possible. The Berkeley Public Library was very helpful in this regard, but I bought a few scores I wanted to mark up: the Mahler Seventh Symphony, for example, which I bought in a reprint of an early edition, then laboriously annotated to incorporate changes the composer had made for the final version.

We finally were able to afford a tape recorder, too, a second-hand Viking model, and I recorded broadcasts of new music from KPFA in order to study them more carefully. Alas, the heads on this machine were out of alignment, and all those recordings had to be scrapped later on.

Duncan Pierce, who had played piano for me in *Camino Real*, lived a few blocks up the street, with his dancer wife and their two kids, and I occasionally visited him, though he moved in circles by then too Bohemian for my taste. Once I rang his doorbell and, hearing him invite me in, went into the house to find him sitting in the dark, the phonograph playing Bartók's *Concerto for Orchestra*. When I asked what he was doing, he replied simply that he was listening to music — teaching me something I'd never considered about the idea of focussing your attention on what you're hearing.

Duncan had an eccentric friend who lived two blocks up Channing from us, Nick Story, a little older than us, a painter who worked as a draftsman for the Chevron plant in Richmond, where fertilizers and pesticides were manufactured. And Kendall was another friend who we often saw; he came to dinner, and stayed for long talk-sessions with the cheap red wine we bought in a bring-your-own-jug store down in South Berkeley.

Duncan worked at the University, giving piano lessons, probably for UC Extension classes, and he told me one day that the University was about to sell off a number of practice pianos, probably at the time the old practice rooms were about to be demolished to make way for the then-new Student Union and Auditorium building. He arranged to have one of them delivered to his house, and I gave him a hard-saved hundred dollars for it, and rented a piano dolly for another dollar or so, and one fine afternoon Duncan and Kendall and I pushed the piano along the sidewalk from his house to ours, stopping briefly at Nick's to play something for him. It was a pretty good piano, an upright Baldwin; it had had a player-piano mechanism at one time, but that had long since been removed; the bass strings were nicely resonant and it didn't take much to put it in tune. We muscled it up the front steps and into the living room, where I set it end-to against one long wall, making a sort of room divider, concealing the sounding board and its ribs with a couple of yards of burlap that I stapled on.

I never really practiced the piano, of course, but picked out some Mozart and Schubert and Bach; and at the piano worked at a little piece for piano and violin. I'd heard somewhere of Darius Milhaud's string octet composed of two string quartets that could be played simultaneously or independently, and I tried to do something of the sort on a much smaller scale; but though the piano part seemed to have some coherence without the violin, writing a piece for unaccompanied violin was utterly beyond my skill or imagination. I did manage to hear one performance, for somehow Duncan cajoled two musicians who had a sympathy for new music to come to our house and give it a reading. I had no idea at the time how unusual this was, or how important the performers were: Robert Bloch, who went soon to UC Davis to help found a newly revitalized music department, and Nathan Schwartz, who would premiere my piano concerto in another six or seven years. They were very generous to try out this naive little piece, crabbed and dense as I recall and undoubtedly beholden to Bartók, whose *Allegro barbaro* I had heard Duncan play in a recital at the University — a performance made memorable by the piano's tendency to move away from him as he played, so that he had to hitch up his piano-stool with his left hand every now and then when the music permitted.

Duncan did what he could to advance my musical taste and understanding. He had an uncle who was somehow involved in public relations for Columbia Records, for example, and was able to get for me the Columbia recording of the complete works (as then known) of Anton Webern, whose music had totally mystified me when I heard a program of his chamber music at UC Berkeley. I played the Columbia recordings over and over, hoping in some way to comprehend the music by assimilation: though it remained enigmatic, the sounds of its utterly clear linear processes became quite familiar and, thereby, attractive.

I'd built my first serious bookcase on half of one long wall in the living room, drilling one-inch holes in one-by -four pine boards, threading them on one-inch dowels that served as uprights, and driving nails through the dowels to serve as pins, holding the shelves up from below. On these were ranged the books: Beckett and Joyce, Virginia Woolf and Dorothy Richardson, a few books of literary criticism; the Penguin books on *The Concerto* and *The Symphony*, a book about conducting; Emily Dickinson. Two sets of four-inch shelves sufficed, one in front of the other, for the upper stages, and before long a third partial set took place in front to give enough depth for the rapidly growing collection of LP records.

For a long while, though, the records sat in wooden boxes on the floor, and one evening when Kendall was over and we'd all had a little too much wine he began dancing about to a recording of the Offenbach *Gaîté Parisienne* suite, and came down hard on a corner of one of the boxes, breaking his leg. He was in a cast and on crutches for a month or so, and as far as I know has never danced since.

My brother Jim was in Berkeley at this time, living in his turn with our grandparents in order to escape the abusive relationship into which our parents' marriage had degenerated. We didn't see much of Mom or my brothers, and virtually nothing of Dad. I don't think I was really aware of quite how trying her life had become, or how marginal and really endangered my brothers' lives were becoming. For one thing, Lindsey's family had quite replaced my own in my affections and normal relationships, even though they were distant by a two-hour drive. For another, Mom made certain not to let me get involved with what she saw as her own problem.

I suppose she may have been more affected than I was, even, by my disastrous first marriage, and she wanted to be sure that nothing she was responsible for would threaten the stability of this one. This was heroic of her, for she suffered a lot, both physically through Dad's battering and badgering, and emotionally through her own hardships, those that had been imposed by circumstances beyond her control, and those that may have been brought on by her own rather obdurate response to her situation.

Marriages were in general more difficult, apparently more troubled than I'd realized. At our own second anniversary dinner party, Nick and Sonny Story announced their decision to divorce. Not long after, Duncan left Luisa, and moved to San Francisco: before long he would be seeing Lindsey's sister, who'd settled in her own apartment there. Arlyn, though, had married a quiet, warm, intelligent architecture student; that marriage was very sound, and she and Chris were good friends, with children of their own.

In any case Jim visited now and then, and one day he brought a friend who was an artist; and while Lindsey sat in our big Mission-style armchair this fellow made a portrait of Lindsey in pastels, on a big sheet of butcher paper. We still have the portrait; I couldn't work at a desk without it near. Shortly after he finished it I took it to Contemporary Arts, on Shattuck Avenue, to have it framed; it's never had glass on it, though it has been sprayed with fixative, and one of these days I mean to have it taken proper care of...

For a year or so I continued to work at the post office, throwing bundles of letters into this sack or that, or sitting long hours at a vertical sorting-case and distributing letters via various routes to cities all over the world. Occasionally I'd be sent down to Oakland to work in the huge parcel distribution center, in those days in a wreck of a warehouse near the old railroad station, but most of the time I worked in the main Post Office in Berkeley, across from the YMCA in whose pool I'd learned to swim ten or twelve years before, when I was going to Garfield Junior High.

There were some friendly fellows at work. I particularly remember a Japanese-American clerk named Kenji, who worked the high-status airmail and special delivery cases; and a very stout fellow named Austin, whose spare-time enthusiasm was for Greek and Russian liturgical music, and who had little good to say about my own musical enthusiasms.

("Gerswine," he said disgustedly once, when the background-music radio drifted into the Piano Concerto, on one of the rare occasions we'd managed to switch it from Muzak to "classical." There were many fights over that radio, culminating one day in my sneaking in to drench it thoroughly in a bucket of water.)

And there was a taciturn, almost morose fellow, Vladimir Drozdoff, the son of Russian immigrants, who was married to a Greek-American woman of amazing tragic beauty, and who had two children: we became close friends. There was a postal clerk named Glen Edwards who I enjoyed for what seemed his deep knowledge of all things Greek. He was obsessed with Greece, and hoped one day to go there, though his wife forbade it, citing his children's dependence on them. One day, though, he could stand it no longer and announced he was leaving. He booked a flight on Icelandic Airlines, but on arriving at the Luxembourg airport remorse set in, and he turned right around and flew back — to find that his wife had packed up the kids and left, and would never speak to him again.

In those days we did not go to restaurants, and rarely to concerts or movies. We had no television. On days off I'd start the day, particularly if the weather was fine, with a loud Mahler symphony, and perhaps if there was time we'd go up to the campus for a picnic, or friends would come over for conversation over a bottle of wine.

And I was attending classes, finally, at the University of California in Berkeley — the fourth college I was to attend. My grades had steadily improved as the courses I took had converged with my interests, from a mediocre record at High School, through average grades (except in music) at Chapman, to quite good grades in English classes (though not in philosophy!) at State, and consequently, I think, I was allowed to enter Cal.

I thought briefly of declaring a music major, but I was scared of the placement exams in theoretical subjects, which really didn't interest me. So I declared a major in my second love, English literature. Even there I had to deal with periods that had no interest for me at all — Pope and Swift, for example — but I enjoyed a class in medieval English literature given by the great and inspiring teacher James Cline, who could keep a large class riveted in awe and admiration when he paced the floor reciting passages from Hakluyt; and another in Chaucer given by Alain Renoir.

And here I met a young teacher's assistant, Alva Bennett, who became a close friend for a number of years. He was a graduate student in Classics and particularly devoted to one of the most brilliant members of the faculty at that time, Elroy Bundy. Bundy was legendary. He had been a lumberjack, it was said, and a boxer; he was devoted to the most notoriously difficult of Greek literature; and he was a sportsman. One day when I was failing first-semester Latin under his care — through no fault of his, but my own laziness and inattention — he asked how I expected to pass the class.

"I'll study hard and get an A in the final," I told him, "and that will give me a passing grade for the course."

"If you get an A in the final," Bundy said, "you'll get an A in the course." I was delighted until he continued: "And if you get anything less than an A in the final, you'll fail the course."

Lindsey and I worked hard at the flashcards, I got an A in the final, I got an A in the course, and I remember virtually nothing of my Latin. I remember considerably more of Bundy, who I once saw make a perfect Massee shot on a pool table at the Blue Cue on Telegraph Avenue, during the brief respectable popularity of the game in the early Sixties.

I was particularly lucky to be at the University, I suppose, on one occasion: we'd bought enough woven sea-grass twelve-inch squares to carpet the living room, and were installing them, when I accidentally plunged a knife onto the palm of my left hand, severing a nerve to one of my fingers. We rushed to the student health service, then at Cowell Hospital, where not knowing my inoculation records I was given a healthy shot of horse serum lest I develop a tetanus reaction. Instead I reacted dramatically to the horse serum, developing a massive case of hives and an inflammation of the pericardium. I spent a week in the hospital and another week or two in bed at home. This had happened just as I was taking final exams, and I was feverish and probably a little deranged during one exam in particular, causing me to fail the exam and therefor barely pass the course in what had been a particularly interesting class in English poetry, taught by the fascinating Willard Farnham, whose enchanting lectures ranged easily from Laurence Sterne to Gertrude Stein.

Needing some easier courses than the strenuous classes in Latin and English literature I took two music classes. One was perhaps useful, a class in orchestration given by one of the faculty celebrities, Joaquín Nin-Culmell. He was short and stocky, with the broad forehead and shoulders typical of some Spanish stock, and he was the brother of the famed diarist Anaïs Nin.

The university Music Department was notoriously Francophile and Germanophobe in those days; the twelve-tone school was not particularly appreciated; and Nin-Culmell assigned us such things as Debussy's *Petite Suite*, in its piano transcription, to adapt to instrumental combinations, then revealing the transcriptions one or another master had made of the same material, to our invariable shame. He asked to see our orchestral compositions, and I'd made a terrible mistake, he said, in asking for simultaneous strokes on the kettledrum and the bass drum: when I showed him examples of that very error in scores by Berlioz and Rossini he was unimpressed.

More shameful was my signup for a class in the appreciation of twentieth-century music — after all, I had learned a great deal about it already from Gunther Schuller's radio broadcasts. This was given by Lawrence Moe, who struck me as humorless and doctrinaire, but the class was undemanding and contributed easily to the improvement of my grades. In the spring of 1960 I was startled to discover I was only a few credits short of graduating, and in one feverish burst of summer school I completed the two classes remaining: a survey of Shakespeare, which required reading thirteen plays (and writing about them) in six weeks, and, much worse, the second semester of Freshman English, which I could not escape, though I was by now older than the teacher, a young novelist named Frederick Crews, and had clearly proved I could read and write acceptable English, the only goal of the class.

A month or two later, in February, 1960, Paolo was born — named for Paul Buonaccorsi, of course, and to celebrate Lindsey's Italian heritage: if he'd been a girl he'd have been Francesca — and it was clear we'd soon outgrow our quarters on Channing Way. By now we'd learned how to hunt for an apartment: we simply checked the ads in the Co-op News. The Berkeley Co-op was perhaps the most significant part of our social life in those days, an institution that had taken root at the heart of Berkeley's socially conscious citizenry in the early

1940s, and seemed likely to live forever — a moral and social governor of sorts, tolerant enough for the religious right, typified by my grandparents, who faithfully shopped Co-op all their lives, and the Communist left. It began in a single location, on University Avenue, midway — significantly — between the hard-drinking bayfront Berkeley below San Pablo Avenue and the enlightened, intellectual (though hardly less alcoholic) campus community in the hills. But by the late 1950s it had built another huge center on Shattuck Avenue near Vine Street, tearing out some old twostorey brownshingle houses including the one whose backyard railroad train had enthralled me a dozen years earlier.

Berkeley: Francisco Street

And it was near this Co-op that we were to find our next home, another duplex, again on the north side of the street guaranteeing light-filled rooms, a stucco vaguely "Venetian" style building whose living quarters were perched, Italian-style, on the second floor, over a street-level garage with a large utility room behind it.

I panelled that room and cleaned it up a bit and installed my studio: the piano; my books; a desk and drafting table. I still hadn't committed myself fully, either to music or to literature. I painted a little and even tried my hand at sculpture, and I thought I needed a lot of room for these activities. We installed our big brass bed in the living room, for some reason, and put Thérèse and Paolo in the one bedroom, at the back of the house.

We still have some of the stuff I made in those years. There's a big white-on-white painting, for example, in our hall: if you were to take it down you'd find on the other side of the canvas an almost completed painting of a nude woman in the familiar old basket chair, holding an orange enigmatically in her outstretched hand. Perched on our present bookcase, here in the study as I write this, is a small assemblage-sculpture I made: *Self-portrait as Napoleon protecting his wife and daughter.* I was growing more and more interested in Dada and Surrealism.

Lindsey's mother had given us a magnificent dining set — a round walnut table and four or five chairs — and over it we hung a fine round globe of a chandelier, bought at the posh furniture store Fraser's on Telegraph Avenue. Even though the bed was in the living room, it was possible to entertain: but before long it was clear a better solution involved making a dormitory for the kids downstairs, moving our bed to the bedroom where it belonged, and beginning to live like mature grownups. I gave up sculpture and painting, left the piano downstairs, and moved the drafting table upstairs to a little breakfast-room, nicely lit by east-facing windows, and big enough too for most of the bookcase salvaged from Channing Way.

By now I'd left the post office, after an unbroken stretch of two or three years' employment — my longest such stretch to date — and taken a job with the City of Berkeley. I think I'd done this because it paid better, but I'm not sure. For the first couple of days I worked with a sewer crew, whose usual job it was to clear out obstructed sewers. At the time, though, some emergency repairs were being made to one of the long underground tunnels that took Strawberry Creek under a number of blocks of downtown Berkeley, from the University campus until it came back to daylight near the University Avenue Co-op.

These tunnels were by then nearly a hundred years old in places, made of concrete, often poured in place over stone-and-concrete floors. The floors were giving way, allowing the creek to wash out around the tunnels, endangering overhead building, and it was our job to repair these floors. The creek would be temporarily diverted for a few dozen feet at a time, allowing the floor to be re-paved; and I was one of the laborers whose job it was to bring wheelbarrowloads of wet concrete from the nearest access manhole, where it was sumped through a chute into our waiting wheelbarrows which we then trundled down the bumpy wet floor to wherever the repair was being made.

This was hard enough, but even harder because the ceiling was so low — a man's height at the time the tunnel was built, several generations before mine, when laborers were considerably less than six feet tall. After a couple of days of this my hands were so blistered I could no longer safely manage the wheelbarrow, and I was transferred to another unit to give them time to callous over. This was a sidewalk crew, and I worked happily with this crew for the next year, usually assigned to the sledge hammer: I broke up sidewalks and removed the broken concrete to a waiting dump truck, then dug out the resulting mess to a uniform three-inch depth between form boards, then wheelbarrowed the fresh concrete in. More expert workers than I built the forms and troweled the concrete.

I'd started this job while we were still on Channing Way, and continued it after our move. Lindsey packed a lunch for me every morning, often liverwurst and raw-onion sandwiches, sometimes wrapping a cold can of beer in aluminum foil to keep it cold through the morning. After years at the post office, breathing dust and listening to either noisy machinery or junk radio stations, this job was a joy: I was out in the fresh air; I grew stronger and more sure of myself physically. Rainy weather was of course a nuisance, but that didn't happen too often. The other guys on the crew, nearly all of them black, made fun of me at first, ridiculing my spoken English with its sounded "g" on gerunds, for example, and looking askance at lunchtime when I'd read a book instead of joining in on conversations about things I found incomprehensible. But I could carry four eighty-pound sacks of cement at a time, two under each arm; I'd learned how to wield a sledge hammer and a pickax; and no one picked a fight with me.

Unfortunately the job wouldn't last more than a year. The

administration wanted me to rise through the ranks, becoming first a supervisor, then probably go into the office. This I would not do. I didn't want a supervisor's responsibility; I didn't want to study and take contracting tests; I wanted to be left alone to do my unskilled work during the day and study and write and enjoy myself on my own time.

By now Kendall had married his pretty young dancing girl and they'd gone off to New York where she hoped to build a career. Kendall had been giving recorder lessons to a few faculty wives and he turned them over to me. We spent a year or so scrimping by, Lindsey doing some child-care, me working at occasional odd jobs and giving recorder lessons. It was a hard time, not made easier by the arrival of Giovanna on New Year's Day, 1963.

She came home without a name — it was hard to find the right one to follow Thérèse and Paolo. It didn't seem right to name siblings Paolo and Francesca. One day the home nurse came by and told us the City would name her if we didn't; she couldn't go through life called Baby Girl Shere. So Giovanna Maddalena it was, for my cousin Joanne, recalled fondly from my earliest childhood (though never seen since my Junior High days) and for Madeleine the heroine of my failed novel *Early Twilight, Early Dawn*; and Giovanna she has remained, and the name seems perfect.

A lot of my spare time, and most of my musical activity, was devoted to the recorder. I had a special friend in Charles Watson, a good-natured, reserved, musical, and very intelligent black guy who had worked with me at the post office. He and his friend, a small, very dark-complexioned, elegant man named Herbert, joined Arlyn Christopherson and me and one of my students, Audrey Kursinski, in a quintet; we got together every week or so, and once even gave a concert in the AME Church in South Berkeley. I don't recall writing much music after that abortive piece for violin and piano, but I did make some arrangements for this recorder ensemble, and sketched out a setting of some text or other — I don't recall what — for tenor, recorder, and piano, an unlikely combination.

By now, too, I was playing the cello. Well, perhaps "playing" is too strong a word: I was playing at it. Somewhere I'd met an older man, Ed Nylund, a cellist who worked in Oakland as a music librarian, a man with an alarmingly German Expressionist face, wrinkled in lines of perpetual astonished anxiety. He took me under his wing, sensed my purposelessness, and told me I'd better amount to something by the time I was thirty, or I'd never amount to anything at all. He found a cello for me and offered to give me lessons, but practice bored me. He forgave that, sensing my preference for composition, and proceeded to explain matters of musical theory to me, using a kind of structural analysis that immediately appealed to me.

I'd never been interested in harmony and counterpoint, the two aspects of conventional "classical" music theory that traditionally form the bedrock of serious musical study. I had always been interested in two other aspects: orchestration, which studies the actual sensual sounds of music; and form, which has to do with the architecture of a composition, the relationships among its components. Harmony and counterpoint are grammars of music; orchestration is inflection; form is poetics.

Ed's method of analysis was reductionist, I suppose, in its simplest extreme content to divide musical gestures into two types: precedent and consequent. But it had the virtue of clarifying connections between small things — groups of only three or four notes, perhaps — and large sections of a long musical composition. (It also, I realize as I write this, relates to other similar processes of analysis and categorization that have fascinated me since: Christopher Alexander's "grammar" of architecture in *The Timeless Way of Building*; Carol Braider's book *The Grammar of Cooking*.)

with Lindsey and Giovanna, summer 1963

8: Sabbatical Year, 1963-1964

ALL THIS MUSICAL ACTIVITY BEGAN to crowd in on my free time, and a few months after Giovanna was born one of my recorder students, Edith Fitzell, made us a gift that truly changed the direction of our lives. Sensing that I needed to focus on a serious choice as to career she gave us a check for two thousand dollars. This enabled me to quit my job with the City of Berkeley. If Lindsey did a little baby-sitting and I did a few odd jobs, and continued giving recorder lessons, we would be able to get by for an entire year, while I took serious studies in music, finally proving whether it was indeed the correct choice. This was a little frightening: if it turned out wrong, I had no idea where I'd go next. After graduating from UC Berkeley, finally, in the summer of 1960, I'd tried graduate school twice: once for a very short time in Library School, which proved too focussed on procedural mechanics for my taste; another time in a program being developed to provide the state with a large number of provisionally credentialed highschool teachers — but hiring interviews with one or two highschool principals soon showed me that the requirements of curriculum and educational approach would never conform to my instincts for anarchy and improvisation.

Let it be music, then: and I began studies, private lessons with Gerhard Samuel, who then conducted the Oakland Symphony. The first lesson was discouraging for both of us, I'm sure. He went to the piano and played four notes, one after another, and asked me to identify them. I couldn't. They were G,

D, A, and E; the open strings of a violin. Well, no matter, let's work on them, he said, and before long they were burned into my mind, and we went on to more interesting things.

I think he must have known I was not a performer, that I lacked every performing instinct. I would not practice; I didn't play piano; I hadn't touched a violin since I was seven years old. But clearly I did have some musical qualities; while he never praised them to me, I heard from others that he'd recommended me to them.

My "studies" with him involved attending all the rehearsals of the Oakland Symphony, listening for balances in every part of the hall, getting to know the music being prepared — not only from the score, which provided the notes and the form, but from the rehearsals, which revealed the importance of situational negotiations on such things as tempo and volume, the prominence of this group of instruments or that, the psychology of communication as conductor, section leader, or instrumentalist — not to mention the composer! — adjusted their various individual takes on the music to the evolving group process by which it came to life, finally, before an audience of two thousand people.

Once, fairly soon after beginning with Gary, I was able to find out for myself how much of a performer I might be. Duncan Pierce had introduced me to a friend, Carolyn Hawley, a pianist then working on the exotic music of Olivier Messiaen, and also a composer. She had written a trio for the improbable combination of flute, guitar, and piano, and it proved to be too difficult to throw together for the annual concert of student compositions programmed at the University on the free Wednesday Noon Concert series. She asked me to conduct it, co-ordinating the rehearsals and keeping it together in performance. Somehow I managed to get through the assignment, but while I took some pride in the experience there was little pleasure.

The early lessons with Gary were in his home in the Oakland hills, a tastefully furnished "ranch house" he'd named Villa Orpheus. The orchestral rehearsals were in the old Auditorium Theater, a fine small cube of a hall providing wonderful acoustics to an audience of two thousand. The first time I attended a rehearsal I think Gary introduced me to the orchestra, simply by way of explaining a stranger in their midst with no instrument in his hands. I was asked to turn pages for one of the bassoonists, who for some reason was playing not from his own part but from an orchestral score. (I later learned he was preparing to audition for Gary's assistant conductor.) Awkwardly approaching an empty chair next to him I stepped on his wallet of spare reeds, lying open on the floor in front of him. I'm sure I smashed two or three. He was quite graceful about it, and later Robert Hughes proved to be an enthusiastic supporter of my music, commissioning in fact two of my best pieces — perhaps more because of his generalized enthusiasm for all things new than for the intrinsic appeal of my own music.

Gary invited me to attend the festival he had co-founded with Hughes and the composer Lou Harrison that year in Aptos, a hundred miles to the south, but I declined to go, thinking it too generous an offer. Gary was enthusiastic about and sympathetic to new regional music, and had asked to see the music I'd written by then. He seemed to like the songs — especially a fairly long one, setting Dylan Thomas's "In my craft and silent art" for voice, recorder, and piano. He showed it to his friend from Minnesota, then recently arrived in California, Robert Erickson. All my composition until then had been one-take improvisation: even the early attempt at intellectual composition, in the *Eight Banalities* for violin and piano, had been written, one by one, in single sittings. If Gary showed me the public and collective process that is musical performance, Bob, as I quickly was asked to address Robert Erickson, showed me the private and individual discipline involved in musical composition. Bob wanted me to undertake a substantial piece, a piece of any kind, for any instrument or group, but a piece whose dimensions would require working at it, setting it aside, mulling it over, resuming it the next day.

This has always been a difficult thing for me. I notice it is difficult for my brothers, too; perhaps there was something in our childhoods that affected our development in this regard. It is difficult at this very moment, as I type the fifty-five thousandth word in this evolving memoir: do I simply continually press forward, occasionally making notes to myself to insert something that's just come to mind in the earlier place where it belongs; or do I go back, revise before finishing, tweak and adjust, and thereby lose the impetus necessary over the long run?

The answer's simple enough, if you're simply a writer (or a composer): you finish a draft, then go back and revise. This was Bob's lesson, and a simple one enough; but he was really the first to give it to me with any clarity — perhaps only because I was only now mature enough to see it, and to have the willingness, however regretful, to set aside undisciplined but seductive irrelevancies in order to get on with it.

(I have more to say about this, which only proves the problem persists as I approach seventy years of age. I am not simply a writer (or composer); I am also a critic, a person who continually has something else come to mind, changing the context or meaning of whatever it is I'm dealing with — or at least my own address to it — and therefor inviting constant revision.)

My first lessons with Bob were in a small studio he'd rented behind a house in the Berkeley hills, up behind the Claremont Hotel. I think he was still teaching at UC Berkeley at the time; or perhaps he'd already moved over to the San Francisco Conservatory. In any case it was private lessons I wanted; I wasn't about to take the placement exams a serious educational institution would require of me. I rationalized this as a stratagem for saving time, as I'd taken a few courses by final exam only while still at UC Berkeley, having lost so much time to various mistakes earlier on. After all, I'd graduated from high school before my seventeenth birthday; why was I still having to go to college as I approached thirty? In fact, though, I'm sure I was too insecure to confront examinations of any kind, afraid that I would fail them, and would be set back once more into a condition of uncertainty, with no clear career, no way of proving myself, no way of providing for my family.

Gary and Bob provided a kind of authoritative support for my instinctive trust in myself, though; and this was supported, in a way, by the tolerance a few real musicians showed for my first fumbling attempts to compose. Phil Lesh turned up again — he'd played trumpet in *Camino Real* — and introduced me to a couple of friends of his, also composing students as well as performing instrumentalists: the pianist Tom Constanten and the percussionist Steve Reich, then driving taxi in San Francisco while studying, I think at the Conservatory. We gathered from time to time in someone's studio in San Francisco, and it was there that we read through a Serenade I was working on — one of a number of pieces I never really finished, as too many things were beginning to happen all at once.

Along with these lessons, I was free now to spend some time going to concerts. I heard the complete *Art of Fugue* in the rococo circular auditorium at San Francisco's Palace of the Legion of Honor, where I was distracted from Margaret Fabrizio's brilliant and dramatic performance at the harpsichord by the peanut-chewing man sitting in front of me — he turned out to be Alfred Frankenstein, the music critic of the San Francisco Chronicle; and he introduced me to the man in the wheelchair in the aisle next to him, Darius Milhaud.

(When I told him shyly that his string octet had inspired me to write a similar piece for violin and piano, and that the piano part could be played alone, he asked, interested, if I could play the violin part without the piano. No, I replied, misunderstanding the question, I can't play the violin at all. We then looked at one another in mutual incomprehension., and conversed only once again, years later)

I heard John Cage and David Tudor, who gave a marvelous but completely mystifying concert that same year, 1963, when the San Francisco Museum of Art invited them to put on a concert in its fourth-floor rotunda. Alfred Frankenstein, always a champion of the *dernier cri*, wrote an advance piece that piqued my curiosity, and we attended. I was completely mystified, I suppose, as to any connection between this event and what I knew to be the tradition of concert music, "classical" music; but the orderly procedures followed by Cage and Tudor as they soberly tickled phonograph needles, rubbed contact microphones over rubber balloons, or poured water into receptacles, in their performances of *Cartridge Music* and one of the *Variations* was clearly, somehow, "musical."

Perhaps most tellingly I heard a concert put on by the radio station KPFA in San Francisco, a concert of pieces that had won a competition they'd sponsored for new compositions: The winner, as I recall, was Pauline Oliveros, with a Trio for violin, piano, and page turner. This inspired me to submit my first really finished piece, a chamber piece for seven instruments to which I'd given the name *Fratture* — in Italian because I'd written it in a class I was taking from Luciano Berio, who alternated with Milhaud teaching composition at Mills College. I ws elated and, in a sense, validated when it won an Honorable Mention; and I was thrilled later when it was played at a contemporary-music festival in Osaka, of all places. (The bilingual program was funny, for the program note I'd been asked to supply had been translated into Japanese, then back again into a sort of English.)

I'd been invited to audit Berio's composition seminar by Phil Lesh, who'd played trumpet in my score for *Camino Real*. I rode out to the Mills campus twice a week, I think, with Phil and his friend Tom Constanten: they sat up front, smoking marijuana and frightening me with their giggles and the prospect that we'd all be arrested for some traffic violation. (We never were.) Berio was elegant, friendly, but frighteningly competent. Once we arrived early and found him writing out a beautiful trio-sonata largo on the blackboard: when I exclaimed at the beauty of the melodic line he said: Like it? I just thought of it. He'd composed it on the spot. I was struck by the power of what I took to be his European conservatory training, and the hopelessness of my ever attaining anything near it.

But it was not counterfeit Bach but authentic Berio that fascinated me. I'd heard his early orchestral work, *Alleluia II*, with its spectacular setting of passages from Joyce, in a KPFA broadcast, and I wanted to hear more. Before long I was rewarded: there was a concert at Mills of his music, including the marvelous song-cycle Circles. This was sung by his wife, the brilliant and beautiful American mezzosoprano Cathy Berberian, who later, in San Francisco, sang the remarkable *Credentials* by Roman Haubenstock-Ramati; and afterward we all went out to Tommy's Joynt for late-night hamburgers and beer.

During this "sabbatical" year we necessarily continued to live very frugally. Lindsey was, and has always remained, masterly at the art of frugal living; without this gift and discipline — for it is both — our lives would have been immensely less rich and rewarding. She made money baby-sitting, and I continued to do the occasional odd job, making frequent trips up to the "Placement Office," the employment bureau the University ran in a wood-frame "temporary building" right at the center of campus, to get a few hours' employment when the larder ran dangerously low, or the rent was unavoidably due. Two or three times I had a job driving an invalid down to Santa Cruz to visit his relatives, but usually the jobs were more mundane: weeding, or painting, or temporary work in one of the bookstores.

Jim and I were shelving books on Bancroft Way when we heard a commotion outside: on going out to see what was happening, we heard that President Kennedy had just been shot in Dallas. The bookstore owner came out to the sidewalk to find out why we weren't working, and we told him the news. Never mind that, he said, get back to work. I quit on the spot.

Jim got me another job that was much more fascinating, working as a night watchman at the Art Festival the San Francisco Art Commission put on every year. Here we huddled in front of a bonfire, making occasional tours on foot through the panels and pavilions temporarily erected on the plaza between City Hall and the Main Library. We had two companions, a poet, Adam David Miller, who was something of a mentor to Jim, and an impressively louche ex-Marine (and, I suspect, a CIA agent) named Charlie Howe. Howe was married to the beautiful daughter of an elegant, slim, courtly Italian, Elio Benvenuto, who had settled in San Francisco, where he made elegant, slim, formal abstract sculpture that had nothing at all in common with the roughly expressionist, mostly quite amateurish stuff exhibited in the Festival.

This job was good for a week or so, and brought in a fair amount of money. And on the final evening, when everything was taken down, we were able to make off with one of the many potted plants that had screened and decorated the show, an olive tree that served as a birthday present for Lindsey. We planted it in front of our duplex on Francisco Street, and it's still there, now grown to an impressive size.

Mrs. Fitzell's gift was meant to allow me to focus on finding a musical career, but it also revealed the immense range of possibilities, and the hardly less immense obstacle my own uncertainties and inadequacies and lack of discipline had created for me. Through it all Lindsey was loyal and faithful, devoted to the three kids, equally to her parents however difficult their own marriage was turning out to be. Weekends on her parents' ranch were wonderful: in the summer we swam in the Russian River, which bordered the ranch, taking picnic lunches with us; occasionally I rode the family nag Black Eagle through the fields; there were long political arguments with Lindsey's father Bob, always loyal to his leftist Seattle past. And we ate well at the ranch, where Agnes's cooking was plain and copious, and we could enjoy fresh fruit and vegetables from the orchards and gardens, and meat from the farm's own pigs and calves, as well as the occasional venison or pheasant provided by a hunting neighbor.

Over the previous year or two, ever since I'd assembled that Heathkit FM tuner, the Berkeley radio station KPFA had been important to both Lindsey and me — to her for its public-affairs programming, which provided every possible point of view on pressing social and political issues; to us both for its coverage of music and particularly contemporary music. There were performances, recorded live, of contemporary music by Dutch and Swedish and Japanese composers, performed at festivals in those countries; and the marvelous series of programs produced in New York by the composer Gunther Schuller, *Contemporary Music in Evolution*, which simply presented pathbreaking compositions chronologically, a year at a time, thereby juxtaposing Ravel (for example) and Schoenberg, Webern and Bartók. Here was another way of revealing affinities and groupings, of suggesting a nonverbalizable kind of meaningful content within a fluctuating ("evolving" seems too pointed a word) cultural context. The music delighted and intrigued; even more, the possibility of this greater or more basic meaning was seductive. At one point there was a strike at KPFA, and we drove back from the ranch with sacks of oranges from its trees to distribute among the picketers. I don't recall now who it was we knew there, but friendships developed, with important consequences, as will be seen.

During this sabbatical year I was a frequent browser at Books Unlimited, a retail bookshop run as a co-operative and set up within the Co-op supermarket on Shattuck Avenue. Here as usual I was attracted to modernist literature and eccentric typography. Among my discoveries I was particularly delighted with the Yale University Press series of Gertrude Stein's work, then being remaindered and so within my budget, and a little book issued by Cape Goliard Press, a translation of Francis Ponge's *Le savon*, the title wisely translated, simply, as *Soap*.

The manager of the store, Robert Yamada, asked me one day if I would stand for election to its board of directors, and without any opposition I was easily elected. One of the other directors proved to be the pianist Julian White, who I'd met years earlier when he lived in a furnished room next door to Kendall's. (He had nearly driven poor Kendall crazy, in fact, with his constant practice, particularly of Schumann.) Julian had a far-ranging cultural interest, however, and was a voracious reader as well as a thoughtful musician, and conversations with him were enlightening and entertaining, challenging me to take another look at the nineteenth century, at German romanticism, and at the great American literature of the mid-century: work by Emerson and Thoreau and Hawthorne.

Toward the end of 1963 I discovered a text translation and book-form realization that George Wittenborn had published of the notes Marcel Duchamp had published in 1934, the "Green Box," notes accompanying his painting *La mariée mise à nu par ces célibataires, même*, a fascinating little book filled with odd typography, drawings, diagrams, and a few photographs of the original notes. Perhaps coincidentally Duchamp's first retrospective was then up, curated by Walter Hopps in the old Pasadena Art Museum, as Lindsey discovered one day in the newspaper. I've described elsewhere, in *How I Saw Duchamp*, how we borrowed Mom's car and drove down to Pasadena in time to see the show on its last day. I'm not sure if I described in that lecture, however, just what it was about the *Bride*, to use the short title, that so fascinated me. I think it was the elusive nature of the content of the work, which is not simply visual and inherent in the painting, complex as it is in its mixed media and considerable transparency; nor simply literary in the Mallarmé-like prose poetry of Duchamp's notes; nor purely intellectual in spite of the considerable commentary that was beginning to grow up around it, and was for that matter implicit in some of the evident philosophical and linguistic and even mathematical allusions of Duchamp's own words, playful as they were.

> *The machine with 5 hearts, the pure*
> *child of nickel and platinum must*
> *dominate the Jura-Paris road. ...*

What fascinated me most about all this was that there was in Duchamp's work, as there was in Mallarmé's and, I thought by then, in Cage's — and perhaps in Webern's for that matter — a "meaning" that could be pondered, discussed, and even related to my own personal experience, but a "meaning" that was ineffably unstateable in purely prosaic terms. I recognize that this concept is mystical and romantic, but I can't help it: it was the conclusion to which I was tending then, as my sabbatical year was allowing me to find my own mature way of applying the child I had been to the adult world in which I was taking my place.

And particularly to the world of Modernism as applied not to politics but to Art, for here I sensed the categories were breaking down; painters and writers and composers were discovering shared insights into human expression and experience that seemed more basic, more "natural," than the traditional intellectual disciplines that had gathered over the centuries, become particularly entrenched in the "received knowledge" of schools and critics. So I remember a performance in the patio of the fine old brown-shingle building on the UC Campus then devoted to the Architecture department, and now I think the School of Journalism, in which two young UC students, Terry Riley and La Monte Young, performed actions of an abstract but expressive nature which lay somewhere between dance, theater, and music. On another occasion LaMonte gave a one-hour program of his own work at one of the free Noon Concerts in the then fairly new Hertz Hall on the campus: one piece involved simply sliding chairs across the stage; another consisted in the release of butterflies. A prominent philosophy professor who specialized in aesthetics, Karl Aschenbrenner — did I take a course from him? — was in the audience, and stood up at one point, loudly stated that this was not music, and stalked out.

In the fall of 1963 Robert Erickson and Gerhard Samuel, with the assistance of a young composer my own age named Loren Rush, formed a performing group dedicated to new music, Performers' Choice. They gave two or three programs in the Little Theater at Berkeley High School, broadcast live over KPFA, and though I didn't help in any way in the rehearsals of these concerts, they too contributed to my rapidly expanding experience with new music. Gary had also presented a performance of Pierre Boulez's *Le marteau sans maître* at UC Berkeley, a performance that seemed to me brilliant and which had required, the word went, thirty rehearsals.

Performances like these went a long way to making immediate and practically accessible the New Music that was becoming available on recordings. Columbia Records had followed its release of the Webern album with a series of recordings of new music. An upstart label, Time Records, countered with a series, curated by the New York composer Earle Brown, presenting music by the New York school: Brown, Cage, Morton Feldman, Christian Wolff. There was a phenomenal recording, on Columbia I think, of Karlheinz Stockhausen's *Zeitmasse* and *Refrain*; I listened to this over and over again, internalizing Stockhausen's curiously abrupt lyricism. And Charles Ives was being rediscovered — I wished now that I'd paid closer attention to those manuscripts in Joe Halprin's cottage, but somehow felt it inappropriate to look the boy up again and ask for another look. How often this reticence kept me, over the years, from following an enthusiasm to its logical conclusion!

Looking back on this *annus mirabilis*, this sabbatical year Mrs. Fitzell had so generously and, I might say, perceptively given me, I'm impressed by the wealth of experience so readily available in the San Francisco Bay Area of the time. The five or six years from the election of J.F. Kennedy to, I suppose, the political suppression that followed the FSM demonstrations, were a golden period for artistic expression. San Francisco had none of the second-city inferiority complex that set in later. Ann Halprin in dance, Allen Ginsburg in poetry, Michael McClure in poetry and theater, Ramon Sender and Pauline Oliveros in music, and any number of other young artists were fusing breakthroughs in technology, in global travel, in new kinds of sensory perception, with a suddenly quite changed understanding of the histories of their arts. Romanticism, Surrealism, Dada, Theater of the Absurd, Existentialism, and the new eclectic lyricism of The Beatles combined with the strong native California sensibility so clearly described, I would find years later, in William Everson's *Archetype West*.

It was a confused and confusing time, but there were guides. Erickson guided a number of us, in the composition seminar he'd recently installed at the San Francisco Conservatory and which he generously made available to me: here we excitedly discussed Terry Riley's recent breakthrough piece *In C*, which we could soon hear in a performance by Gary's Oakland Symphony, and whose premiere performance, at the Conservatory, Frankenstein reviewed as the most significant piece of new music since Stravinsky's *Le sacre du printemps*. Frankenstein himself was another important guide, a popularizer who may not always have understood every aspect of the work he discussed but whose sympathies were always favorable, whose intuitions were always responsive, to any new expression that came his way. Artists thought he was more competent as a music critic; musicians thought him more qualified as an art critic; but members of both groups were grateful for his determination that the conventional traditions and repertoires be extended to include the work being produced at the moment, in the area.

Going to Buffalo

One of the composers I'd been struck by, in programs on KPFA, was the German avant-gardist Karlheinz Stockhausen, and in the winter of 1963 I heard or read that he was in residence at the Buffalo campus of New York State University, where he was preparing the premiere of an important new piece for chorus and orchestra. I determined that I had to attend this, however it could be managed, and together with my brother Jim set off across the country in January 1964. There was no question of our driving; our car wasn't up to that long a trip. I found an ad on the Co-op bulletin board posted by a young graduate student in anthropology: he was looking for someone to share expenses on a drive to New York.

We drove the southern route, out highway 66 to Oklahoma City, then continuing east through Little Rock, Memphis, finally up through Knoxville and the Appalachians to Pittsburgh. The driver slept in motels; we slept in the car, once at a YMCA, in Amarillo, for the much-needed shower. The driver was apparently gathering material for some kind of research, and we went through a number of small towns in Tennessee and northern Mississippi and Alabama, where he would ask the proprietors of local diners whether they served Negros. Jim and I quickly learned not to accompany him on these expeditions, making do with cheese and crackers in the car.

He dropped us in Pittsburgh and we got somehow to Buffalo, New York, arriving at six o'clock or so in the morning of a bitterly cold day. We killed a couple of hours in an earlymorning coffee joint, where I first heard The Beatles on the juke box; and then we somehow got over to the university campus, where accommodations had been arranged for us, for I had asked the music director of KPFA if I might prepare a report on this event, and he had arranged some kind of housing, as well as other press courtesies. We visited the university art museum, with its imposing collection of Paul Klees; and we met Stockhausen, and attended the rehearsals and, finally, the premiere of his *Momente*, a piece whose fascinating sounds and carefully constructed architecture spoke volumes to me.

We tried to hitchhike, after that performance, from Buffalo to New York, but were stopped by police from one jurisdiction after another — city police, state troopers, even finally federal immigration folks. We must have been a pretty disreputable-looking pair, Jim and I; and finally we had to spend almost our last nickels on a Greyhound bus to New York City, where I hoped to be bailed out by Kendall, who was still there though his marriage to the dancing girl had failed; or perhaps by Lindsey's sister Pat, who was newly installed in New York with her new husband Michael, who she'd met on the boat coming back from France.

To an extent this worked out. I crashed with Kendall for a few days; I don't know where Jim stayed — it would be interesting to have his recollections of this trip! Pat and Michael treated me to dinner in a Greek restaurant somewhere, and introduced me to Lindsey's cousin Ivan, a painter who lived with his beautiful wife somewhere in Greenwich Village, not far from Kendall. (We still have a small painting Ivan gave me then, an expressionist self-portrait.) And Kendall, who was working as an accountant, lent me an unheard-of amount of money, one hundred dollars, to finance our return trip to Berkeley, otherwise unprovided for.

I looked at the classified ads for a "driveaway." In those days it occasionally transpired that someone would need a car driven across the country. The only one to be found was a fairly new convertible. I would have to pay for the gas; the use of the car was my compensation for delivering it safely at its destination — in this case, somewhere on the San Francisco peninsula. Jim and I tossed our duffelbags in the trunk and drove off the first day for Washington D.C.: this was technically forbidden as it did not lie on a direct route, but we thought we'd get away with it.

We spent the night with Lindsey's uncle "Rip" — he never went by his real name, which was Othmar. He was Ivan's father, an amateur painter himself, and a labor organizer. He showed us Washington D.C., gave us a bed and breakfast, and saw us off next morning.

Since we had no money we had to sleep in the car, and since our route took us through freezing weather we slept as little as possible. Jim did not know how to drive, so I drove straight through, across Maryland, along the Ohio River, and into Indiana, where I finally could drive no further: I had to sleep. In a few hours I woke up in the midst of a snowfield: only the telegraph wires and an occasional truck, turned over on its side, showed where the highway was. I remember seeing dark objects up the road, scattered about these trucks, and discovering, when we finally got near them, that they were the carcasses of pigs, frozen in the snow — I thought briefly of tossing one into the trunk, to take home for meat.

It was cold enough for that, God knows. It was too cold to sleep in a parked car, so we pressed on, stopping next somewhere in Nevada, again for a few hours of sleep before the final descent, without the required snow chains — we had enough money for chains or gas, but not both — and with the canvas top freezing to the touch, down the Sierra, through Sacramento, through the Delta, back to Berkeley. California and home had never looked so good.

It had been my first parting from Lindsey for any length of time, about a month altogether, and it was just about the last of that duration, and while the Stockhausen had been an unforgettable experience, and much of the rest of the trip memorable for its own novelty, perhaps the most important lesson was that I did not like being away from her and the children. Here was another complication: how to balance a musical career with a domestic life? Erickson and his wife had no children; Gary was a bachelor; so was Ed Nylund; none of the musicians my own age had serious interests in marriage and children.

The friends we had who were "normal" in this respect were professionals, not artists. Arlyn and Chris lived on his income as an architect beginning a career. Our new friends on Francisco Street, Wayne and Elisa Rosing, lived on his job in some kind of electronic engineering. Even Valodya and Julia got by on his job at the post office, though ultimately his romantic émigré character would take them to a farm in Maine, where she kept things going by teaching school. This problem, the balance of a musical career with a family life, was something I would think about for many years to come.

In the meantime I worked on my report of the Stockhausen premiere. This turned out to be my first attempt to communicate with a public: I wasn't writing a paper for an English teacher, but a journalistic report — not a "review" — of a serious event, new and complex enough to require a certain amount of explanation beyond the simple where-and-when.

I'd taken careful notes on the *Momente* premiere and on returning to Berkeley I lost little time making my radio report. I'm not sure how I knew how to do this: probably simply by having heard so much radio reportage of such events before, on KPFA broadcasts. In any case I typed up a script, reporting on the workshops and rehearsals I'd witnessed; and then reporting on the piece as I'd actually heard it: how it evolved in its setting, on the stage facing its audience, the percussion and keyboards at the front of the stage along with the brilliant and dramatic soprano soloist (Martina Arroyo), the chorus standing in a semicircle behind the instruments. The audience politely applauded when the composer walked out from the wings to begin conducting the piece, and he acknowledged the applause, and turned to his musicians, and suddenly they in turn began to applaud the audience, and the piece had begun.

I described the sounds that followed, and how they were made and how they related to one another. I had the tape recording of the Cologne performance of the same piece, and no doubt quite illegally I spliced appropriate excerpts of it into the recording I narrated of my review; and at the end of the "documentary" report of the Buffalo performance we broadcast the Cologne performance in its entirety.

The result was, I see clearly now, a combination of didactics and criticism , music appreciation and journalistic report; and it set a pattern I would follow in a number of radio programs at KPFA and television programs at KQED. I suppose it reflected the two aptitudes I'd shown so many years earlier, when the test results suggested any career for me would lie in teaching or, perhaps, preaching. It was the first serious such work I had done, and left me both a little exhilarated and a little ashamed of my own audacity. And, I think, it confirmed Mrs. Fitzell's perceptiveness in enabling this amazing year. I thanked her by composing the first music that I still enjoy hearing, *Three Pieces for Piano*, later orchestrated as a *Small Concerto for Piano and Orchestra*.

In May, 1964, attracted by a rare chance to hear one of Charles Ives's orchestral pieces — which, I no longer recall — I drove down the coast to the resort town, as I then thought it, of Ojai, to the three-day music festival given there every Memorial Day weekend. I saved money by avoiding motels and restaurants, spending the nights in my sleeping bag in a campground overlooking the valley and eating from the grocery store at a picnic table; and passed the afternoon and evening in town, attending rehearsals and performances on press credentials again arranged through the San Francisco Chronicle, for Alfred Frankenstein had agreed to consider a review from me — on what basis I cannot now imagine. I wrote the review on returning to Berkeley, and it ran; and I joined Gary Samuel in a discussion of the Ojai Festival and the more extensive one he had initiated the previous year in Aptos, a hundred miles south of Berkeley, on the coast.

In the summer of 1964 the music director of KPFA, Will Ogdon, resigned to take a job in San Diego, where he was to establish the Music Department at a new campus of the University of California. He asked me to take his job. I was flattered, frightened, and overjoyed. I was about to celebrate my twenty-ninth birthday: I'd met Ed Nylund's challenge with a year to spare.

For two years or so I was in heaven, spending days and nights listening to all sorts of music, writing scripts, announcing live concerts, editing the program guide, reviewing books. The Sixties were in full swing; everyone else at the station was concerned about news and politics and social justice and the war and the like; I was immersed in music. I was particularly entranced with Modernism, and sacrificed my job for that commitment — but readily found an even better job at a television station, KQED. There I added the visual arts to my interests, writing and hosting and producing programs about painting and sculpture, Dada and Surrealism; but also about bicycling and gardening. From there I drifted into teaching at Mills College, and then joined the staff of the Oakland *Tribune* as art critic, later music critic, and always in some sense critic-at-large; and always, of course, composing.

But all those years, from the time I turned twenty-nine, are a subject for another day. My youth was over, but maturity had hardly begun. There was still a lot to be learned.

Healdsburg, January-April 2005

This book is set in a computer version of Garamond
it was written and composed in AppleWorks
on a Macintosh computer

and printed for the author at Lulu.com

2007

www.ingramcontent.com/pod-product-compliance
Lightning Source LLC
Chambersburg PA
CBHW030927090426
42737CB00007B/344